Dickens' Stories about Children

Every Child can Read

MAVEN BOOKS

Dickens' Stories about Children
Every Child can Read

Charles Dickens

Edited by

Jesse Lyman Hurlbut

MAVEN BOOKS

Chennai   Trichy   Tirunelveli   New Delhi

MAVEN BOOKS

An Imprint of **MJP Publishers**

ISBN 978-93-87488-31-1   **Maven Books**

All rights reserved   No. 44, Nallathambi Street,
Printed and bound in India   Triplicane, Chennai 600 005

MJP 609   © Publishers, 2018

Publisher : C. Janarthanan

Publisher's Note

The legacy of a country is in its varied cultural heritage, historical literature, developments in the field of economy and science. The top nations in the world are competing in the field of science, economy and literature. This vast legacy has to be conserved and documented so that it can be bestowed to the future generation. The knowledge of this legacy is slowly getting perished in the present generation due to lack of documentation.

Keeping this in mind, the concern with retrospective acquiring of rare books has been accented recently by the burgeoning reprint industry. Maven Books is gratified to retrieve the rare collections with a view to bring back those books that were landmarks in their time.

In this effort, a series of rare books would be republished under the banner, "Maven Books". The books in the reprint series have been carefully selected for their contemporary usefulness as well as their historical importance within the intellectual. We reconstruct the book with slight enhancements made for better presentation, without affecting the contents of the original edition.

Most of the works selected for republishing covers a huge range of subjects, from history to anthropology. We believe this reprint edition will be a service to the numerous researchers and practitioners active in this fascinating field. We allow readers to experience the wonder of peering into a scholarly work of the highest order and seminal significance.

Maven Books

PREFACE

TO THE YOUNG READER

Charles Dickens was one of the greatest among the many story-writers of "the Victorian age;" that is, the middle and latter part of the Nineteenth Century, when Victoria was Queen of Great Britain. Perhaps he was the greatest of them all for now, a generation after he passed away, more people read the stories of Dickens than those by any other author of that period. In those wonderful writings are found many pictures of child-life connected with the plan of the novels or stories. These child-stories have been taken out of their connections and are told by themselves in this volume. By and by you will read for yourselves, "The Christmas Carol," "The Chimes," "David Copperfield," "The Old Curiosity Shop," and the other great books by that fascinating writer, who saw people whom [4]nobody else ever saw, and made them real. When you read those books you will meet again these charming children, and will remember them as the friends of your childhood.

JESSE L. HURLBUT

Contents

KNOWLEDGE

I

Trotty Veck and his Daughter Meg

"TROTTY" seems a strange name for an old man, but it was given to Toby Veck because of his always going at a trot to do his errands; for he was a ticket porter or messenger and his office was to take letters and messages for people who were in too great a hurry to send them by post, which in those days was neither so cheap nor so quick as it is now. He did not earn very much, and had to be out in all weathers and all day long. But Toby was of a cheerful disposition, and looked on the bright side of everything, and was grateful for any small mercies that came in his way; and so was happier than many people who never knew what it is to be hungry or in want of comforts. His greatest joy was his dear, bright, pretty daughter Meg, who loved him dearly.

One cold day, near the end of the year, Toby had been waiting a long time for a job, trotting up and down in his usual place before the church, and trying hard to keep himself warm, when the bells chimed twelve o'clock, which made Toby think of dinner.

"There's nothing," he remarked, carefully feeling his nose to make sure it was still there, "more regular in coming round than dinner-time, and nothing less regular in coming round than dinner. That's the great difference between 'em." He went on talking to himself, trotting up and down, and never noticing who was coming near to him.

"Why, father, father," said a pleasant voice, and Toby turned to find his daughter's sweet, bright eyes close to his.

"Why, pet," said he, kissing her and squeezing her blooming face between his hands, "what's to-do? I didn't expect you to-day, Meg."

"Neither did I expect to come, father," said Meg, nodding and smiling. "But here I am! And not alone, not alone!"

"Why you don't mean to say," observed Trotty, looking curiously at the covered basket she carried, "that you———"

"Smell it, father dear," said Meg. "Only smell it!"

Trotty was going to lift up the cover at once, in a great hurry, when she gaily interposed her hand.

"No, no, no," said Meg, with the glee of a child. "Lengthen it out a little. Let me just lift up the corner; just a lit-tle, ti-ny cor-ner, you know," said Meg, suiting the action to the word with the utmost gentleness, and speaking very softly, as if she were afraid of being overheard by something inside the basket. "There, now; what's that?"

Toby took the shortest possible sniff at the edge of the basket, and cried out in rapture:

"Why, it's hot," he said.

But to Meg's great delight he could not guess what it was that smelt so good.

"Polonies? Trotters? Liver? Pigs' feet? Sausages?" he tried one after the other. At last he exclaimed in triumph. "Why, what am I a-thinking of? It's tripe."

And it was.

"And so," said Meg, "I'll lay the cloth at once, father; for I have brought the tripe in a basin, and tied the basin up in a pocket-handkerchief; and if I like to be proud for once, and spread that for a cloth, and call it a cloth, there's nobody to prevent me, is there father?"

"Not that I know of, my dear," said Toby; "but they're always a-bringing up some new law or other."

"And according to what I was reading you in the paper the other day, father, what the judge said, you know, we poor people are supposed to know them all. Ha, ha! What a mistake! My goodness me, how clever they think us!"

"Yes, my dear," cried Trotty; "and they'd be very fond of any one of us that *did* know 'em all. He'd grow fat upon the work he'd get, that man, and be popular with the gentlefolks in his neighborhood. Very much so!"

"He'd eat his dinner with an appetite, whoever he was, if it smelt like this," said Meg cheerfully. "Make haste, for there's a hot potato besides, and half a pint of fresh-drawn beer in a bottle. Where will you dine, father—on the post or on the steps? Dear, dear, how grand we are! Two places to choose from!"

"The steps to-day, my pet," said Trotty. "Steps in dry weather, post in wet. There's greater conveniency in the steps at all times, because of the sitting down; but they're rheumatic in the damp."

"Then, here," said Meg, clapping her hands after a moment's bustle; "here it is all ready! And beautiful it looks! Come, father. Come!"

And just as Toby was about to sit down to his dinner on the door-steps of a big house close by, the chimes rang out again, and Toby took off his hat and said, "Amen."

"They Broke in Like a Grace, My Dear."

"Amen to the bells, father?"

"They broke in like a grace, my dear," said Trotty; "they'd say a good one if they could, I'm sure. Many's the kind thing they say to me. How often have I heard them bells say, 'Toby Veck, keep a good heart, Toby!' A million times? More!"

"Well, I never!" cried Meg.

"When things is very bad, then it's 'Toby Veck, Toby Veck, job coming soon, Toby!'"

"And it comes—at last, father," said Meg, with a touch of sadness in her pleasant voice.

"Always," answered Toby. "Never fails."

While this discourse was holding, Trotty made no pause in his attack upon the savory meat before him, but cut and ate, and cut and drank, and cut and chewed, and dodged about from tripe to hot potato, and from hot potato back again to tripe, with an unfailing relish. But happening now to look all round the street—in case anybody should be beckoning from any door or window for a porter—his eyes, in coming back again, saw Meg sitting opposite him, with her arms folded, and only busy in watching his dinner with a smile of happiness.

"Why, Lord forgive me!" said Trotty, dropping his knife and fork. "My dove! Meg! why didn't you tell me what a beast I was?"

"Father!"

"Sitting here," said Trotty, in a sorrowful manner, "cramming, and stuffing, and gorging myself, and you before me there, never so much as breaking your precious fast, nor wanting to, when——"

"But I have broken it, father," interposed his daughter, laughing, "all to bits. I have had my dinner."

"Nonsense," said Trotty. "Two dinners in one day! It ain't possible! You might as well tell me that two New Year's days will come together, or that I have had a gold head all my life, and never changed it."

"I have had my dinner, father, for all that," said Meg, coming nearer to him. "And if you will go on with yours, I'll tell you how and where, and how your dinner came to be brought and—and something else besides."

Toby still appeared not to believe her; but she looked into his face with her clear eyes, and, laying her hand upon his shoulder, motioned him to go on while the meat was hot. So Trotty took up his knife and fork again and went to work, but much more slowly than before, and shaking his head, as if he were not at all pleased with himself.

"I had my dinner, father," said Meg, after a little hesitation, "with—with Richard. His dinner-time was early; and as he brought his dinner with him when he came to see me, we—we had it together, father."

Trotty took a little beer and smacked his lips. Then he said "Oh!" because she waited.

"And Richard says, father—" Meg resumed, then stopped.

"What does Richard say, Meg?" asked Toby.

"Richard says, father—" Another stoppage.

"Richard's a long time saying it," said Toby.

"He says, then, father," Meg continued, lifting up her eyes at last, and speaking in a tremble, but quite plainly, "another year is nearly gone, and where is the use of waiting on from year to year, when it is so unlikely we shall ever be better off than we are now? He says we are poor now, father, and we shall be poor then; but we are young now, and years will make us old before we know it. He says that if we wait, people as poor as we are, until we see our way quite clearly, the way will be a narrow one indeed—the common way—the grave, father."

A bolder man than Trotty Veck must needs have drawn upon his boldness largely to deny it. Trotty held his peace.

"And how hard, father, to grow old and die, and think we might have cheered and helped each other! How hard in all our lives to love each other, and to grieve, apart, to see each other working, changing, growing old and gray. Even if I got the better of it, and forgot him (which I never could), oh, father, dear, how hard to have a heart so full as mine is now, and live to have it slowly drained out every drop, without remembering one happy moment of a woman's life to stay behind and comfort me and make me better!"

Trotty sat quite still. Meg dried her eyes, and said more gaily— that is to say, with here a laugh and there a sob, and here a laugh and sob together:

"So Richard says, father, as his work was yesterday made certain for some time to come, and as I love him and have loved him full three years—ah, longer than that, if he knew it!—will I marry him on New Year's Day?"

Just then Richard himself came up to persuade Toby to agree to their plan; and, almost at the same moment, a footman came out of the house and ordered them all off the steps, and some gentlemen came out who called up Trotty, and asked a great many questions, and found a good deal of fault, telling Richard he was very foolish to want to get married, which made Toby feel very unhappy, and Richard very angry. So the lovers went off together sadly; Richard looking gloomy and downcast, and Meg in tears. Toby, who had a letter given him to carry, and a sixpence, trotted off in rather low spirits to a very grand house, where he was told to take the letter in to the gentleman. While he was waiting, he heard the letter read. It was from Alderman Cute, to tell Sir Joseph Bowley that one of his tenants named Will Fern, who had come to London to try to get work, and been brought before him charged with sleeping in a shed, and asking if Sir Joseph wished him to be dealt kindly with or otherwise. To Toby's great disappointment, for Sir Joseph had talked a great deal about being a friend to the poor, the answer was given that Will Fern might be sent to prison as a vagabond, and made an example of, though his only fault was that he was poor. On his way home, Toby, thinking sadly, with his hat pulled down low on his head, ran against a man dressed like a country-man, carrying a fair-haired little girl. Toby enquired anxiously if he had hurt either of them. The man answered no, and seeing Toby had a kind face, he asked him the way to Alderman Cute's house.

"It's impossible," cried Toby, "that your name is Will Fern?"

"That's my name," said the man.

Thereupon Toby told him what he had just heard, and said, "Don't go there."

Poor Will told him how he could not make a living in the country, and had come to London with his orphan niece to try to find a friend of her mother's and to endeavor to get some work, and, wishing Toby a happy New Year, was about to trudge wearily off again, when Trotty caught his hand, saying—

"Stay! The New Year never can be happy to me if I see the child and you go wandering away without a shelter for your heads. Come home with me. I'm a poor man, living in a poor place; but I can give you lodging for one night, and never miss it. Come home with me! Here! I'll take her!" cried Trotty, lifting up the child. "A pretty one! I'd carry twenty times her weight and never know I'd got it. Tell me if I go too quick for you. I'm very fast. I always was!" Trotty said this, taking about six of his trotting paces to one stride of his tired companion, and with his thin legs quivering again beneath the load he bore.

"Why, she's as light," said Trotty, trotting in his speech as well as in his gait—for he couldn't bear to be thanked, and dreaded a moment's pause—"as light as a feather. Lighter than a peacock's feather—a great deal lighter. Here we are and here we go!" And, rushing in, he set the child down before his daughter. The little girl gave one look at Meg's sweet face and ran into her arms at once, while Trotty ran round the room, saying, "Here we are and here we go. Here, Uncle Will, come to the fire. Meg, my precious darling, where's the kettle? Here it is and here it goes, and it'll bile in no time!"

"Why, father!" said Meg, as she knelt before the child and pulled off her wet shoes, "you're crazy to-night, I think. I don't know what the bells would say to that. Poor little feet, how cold they are!"

"Oh, they're warmer now!" exclaimed the child. "They're quite warm now!"

"No, no, no," said Meg. "We haven't rubbed 'em half enough. We're so busy. And when they're done, we'll brush out the damp hair; and when that's done, we'll bring some color to the poor pale face with fresh water; and when that's done, we'll be so gay and brisk and happy!"

The child, sobbing, clasped her round the neck, saying, "O Meg, O dear Meg!"

"Good gracious me!" said Meg presently, "father's crazy. He's put the dear child's bonnet on the kettle, and hung the lid behind the door!"

Trotty hastily repaired this mistake, and went off to find some tea and a rasher of bacon he fancied "he had seen lying somewhere on the stairs."

He soon came back and made the tea, and before long they were all enjoying the meal. Trotty and Meg only took a morsel for form's sake (for they had only a very little, not enough for all), but their delight was in seeing their visitors eat, and very happy they were—though Trotty had noticed that Meg was sitting by the fire in tears when they had come in, and he feared her marriage had been broken off.

After tea Meg took Lilian to bed, and Toby showed Will Fern where he was to sleep. As he came back past Meg's door he heard the child saying her prayers, remembering Meg's name and asking for his. Then he went to sit by the fire and read his paper, and fell asleep to have a wonderful dream, so terrible and sad, that it was a great relief when he woke.

"And whatever you do, father," said Meg, "don't eat tripe again without asking some doctor whether it's likely to agree with you; for how you *have* been going on! Good gracious!"

She was working with her needle at the little table by the fire, dressing her simple gown with ribbons for her wedding—so quietly happy, so blooming and youthful, so full of beautiful promise that he uttered a great cry as if it were an angel in his house, then flew to clasp her in his arms.

But he caught his feet in the newspaper, which had fallen on the hearth, and somebody came rushing in between them.

"No!" cried the voice of this same somebody. A generous and jolly voice it was! "Not even you; not even you. The first kiss of Meg in the New Year is mine—mine! I have been waiting outside the house this hour to hear the bells and claim it. Meg, my precious prize, a happy year! A life of happy years, my darling wife!"

And Richard smothered her with kisses.

You never in all your life saw anything like Trotty after this, I don't care where you have lived or what you have seen; you never in your life saw anything at all approaching him! He kept running up to Meg, and squeezing her fresh face between his hands and kissing it, going from her backwards not to lose sight of it, and running up again like a figure in a magic lantern; and whatever he did, he was constantly sitting himself down in his chair, and never stopping in it for one single moment, being—that's the truth—beside himself with joy.

"And to-morrow's your wedding-day, my pet!" cried Trotty. "Your real, happy wedding-day!"

"To-day!" cried Richard, shaking hands with him. "To-day. The chimes are ringing in the New Year. Hear them!"

They *were* ringing! Bless their sturdy hearts, they *were* ringing! Great bells as they were—melodious, deep-mouthed, noble bells, cast in no common metal, made by no common founder—when had they ever chimed like that before?

Trotty was backing off to that wonderful chair again, when the child, who had been awakened by the noise, came running in half-dressed.

"Why, here she is!" cried Trotty, catching her up. "Here's little Lil-ian! Ha, ha, ha! Here we are and here we go. Oh, here we are and here we go again! And here we are and here we go! And Uncle Will, too!"

Before Will Fern could make the least reply, a band of music burst into the room, attended by a flock of neighbors, screaming, "A Happy New Year, Meg!" "A happy wedding!" "Many of 'em!" and other fragmentary good-wishes of that sort. The Drum (who was a private friend of Trotty's) then stepped forward and said:

"Trotty Veck, my boy, it's got about that your daughter is going to be married to-morrow. There ain't a soul that knows you that don't wish you well, or that knows her and don't wish her well. Or that knows you both, and don't wish you both all the happiness the New Year can bring. And here we are to play it in and dance it in accordingly."

Then Mrs. Chickenstalker came in (a good-humored, nice-look-ing woman who, to the delight of all, turned out to be the friend of Lilian's mother, for whom Will Fern had come to look), with a stone pitcher full of "flip," to wish Meg joy, and then the music struck up, and Trotty, making Meg and Richard second couple, led off Mrs. Chickenstalker down the dance, and danced it in a step unknown before or since, founded on his own peculiar trot.

II

Tiny Tim

IT will surprise you all very much to hear that there was once a man who did not like Christmas. In fact, he had been heard on several occasions to use the word *humbug* with regard to it. His name was Scrooge, and he was a hard, sour-tempered man of business, intent only on saving and making money, and caring nothing for anyone. He paid the poor, hard-working clerk in his office as little as he could possibly get the work done for, and lived on as little as possible himself, alone, in two dismal rooms. He was never merry or comfortable or happy, and he hated other people to be so, and that was the reason why he hated Christmas, because people *will* be happy at Christmas, you know, if they possibly can, and like to have a little money to make themselves and others comfortable.

Well, it was Christmas eve, a very cold and foggy one, and Mr. Scrooge, having given his poor clerk permission very unwillingly to spend Christmas day at home, locked up his office and went home himself in a very bad temper, and with a cold in his head. After having taken some gruel as he sat over a miserable fire in his dismal room, he got into bed, and had some wonderful and disagreeable dreams, to which we will leave him, whilst we see how Tiny Tim, the son of his poor clerk, spent Christmas day.

The name of this clerk was Bob Cratchit. He had a wife and five other children besides Tim, who was a weak and delicate little cripple, and for this reason was dearly loved by his father and the rest of the family; not but what he was a dear little boy, too, gentle and patient and loving, with a sweet face of his own, which no one could help looking at.

Whenever he could spare the time, it was Mr. Cratchit's delight to carry his little boy out on his shoulder to see the shops and the people; and to-day he had taken him to church for the first time.

"Whatever has got your precious father and your brother Tiny Tim!" exclaimed Mrs. Cratchit, "here's dinner all ready to be dished up. I've never known him so late on Christmas day before."

"Here he is, mother!" cried Belinda, and "here he is!" cried the other children.

In came little Bob, the father, with at least three feet of comforter, exclusive of the fringe, hanging down before him; and his threadbare clothes darned up and brushed, to look just as well as possible; and Tiny Tim upon his shoulder. Alas for Tiny Tim, he bore a little crutch, and had his limbs supported by an iron frame!

"Why, where's our Martha?" cried Bob Cratchit, looking round.

"Not coming," said Mrs. Cratchit.

"Not coming!" said Bob, with a sudden dropping in his high spirits; for he had been Tim's blood horse all the way from church, and had come home rampant. "Not coming upon Christmas day!"

Martha didn't like to see him disappointed, if it were only in joke; so she came out sooner than had been agreed upon from behind the closet-door, and ran into his arms, while the two young Cratchits hustled Tiny Tim, and bore him off into the wash-house, that he might hear the pudding singing in the copper kettle.

"And how did Tim behave?" asked Mrs. Cratchit.

"As good as gold and better," replied his father. "I think, wife, the child gets thoughtful, sitting at home so much. He told me, coming home, that he hoped the people in church who saw he was a cripple, would be pleased to remember on Christmas day who it was who made the lame to walk."

"Bless his sweet heart!" said the mother in a trembling voice, and the father's voice trembled, too, as he remarked that "Tiny Tim was growing strong and hearty at last."

His active little crutch was heard upon the floor, and back came Tiny Tim before another word was spoken, led by his brother and sister to his stool beside the fire; while Bob, Master Peter, and the two young Cratchits (who seemed to be everywhere at once) went to fetch the goose, with which they soon returned in high procession.

Such a bustle ensued that you might have thought a goose the rarest of all birds; a perfect marvel, to which a black swan was a matter of course—and in truth it was something very like it in that house. Mrs. Cratchit made the gravy (ready beforehand in a little saucepan) hissing hot; Master Peter mashed the potatoes with tremendous vigor; Miss Belinda sweetened up the apple-sauce; Martha dusted the hot plates; Bob took Tiny Tim beside him in a tiny corner at the table; the two young Cratchits set chairs for everybody, not forgetting themselves, and, mounting guard upon their posts, crammed spoons into their mouths, lest they should shriek for goose before their turn came to be helped. At last the dishes were set on, and grace was said. It was succeeded by a breathless pause, as Mrs. Cratchit, looking slowly all along the carving-knife, prepared to plunge it in the breast; but when she did, and when the long-expected gush of stuffing issued forth, one murmur of delight arose all round the board, and even Tiny Tim, excited by the two young Cratchits, beat on the table with the handle of his knife, and feebly cried Hurrah!

There never was such a goose. Bob said he didn't believe there ever was such a goose cooked. Its tenderness and flavor, size, and cheapness were the themes of universal admiration. Eked out by apple-sauce and mashed potatoes, it was a sufficient dinner for the whole family; indeed, as Mrs. Cratchit said with great delight (surveying one small atom of a bone upon the dish), they hadn't ate it all at that! Yet everyone had had enough, and the youngest Cratchits, in particular, were steeped in sage and onions to the eyebrows! But now, the plates being changed by Miss Belinda, Mrs. Cratchit left the room alone—too nervous to bear witnesses—to take up the pudding and bring it in.

Suppose it should not be done enough! Suppose it should break in turning out! Suppose somebody should have got over the wall of the back yard and stolen it, while they were merry with the goose—a supposition at which the two young Cratchits became livid! All sorts of horrors were supposed.

Halloo! A great deal of steam! The pudding was out of the copper. A smell like a washing-day! That was the cloth. A smell like an eating-house and a pastrycook's next door to each other, with a laundress' next door to that! That was the pudding! In half a minute Mrs. Cratchit entered—flushed, but smiling proudly—with the pudding like a speckled cannon-ball, so hard and firm, blazing in half of half-a-quartern of lighted brandy, and decorated with Christmas holly stuck into the top.

Oh, a wonderful pudding! Bob Cratchit said, and calmly too, that he regarded it as the greatest success achieved by Mrs. Cratchit since their marriage. Mrs. Cratchit said that, now the weight was off her mind, she would confess she had her doubts about the quantity of flour. Everybody had something to say about it, but nobody said or thought it was a small pudding for a large family. It would have been really wicked to do so. Any Cratchit would have blushed to hint at such a thing.

At last the dinner was all done, the cloth was cleared, the hearth swept, and the fire made up. The hot stuff in the jug being tasted, and considered perfect, apples and oranges were put upon the table, and a shovel full of chestnuts on the fire. Then all the Cratchit family drew round the hearth in what Bob Cratchit called a circle, meaning half a one; and at Bob Cratchit's elbow stood the family display of glass. Two tumblers and a custard cup without a handle.

These held the hot stuff from the jug, however, as well as golden goblets would have done; and Bob served it out with beaming looks, while the chestnuts on the fire sputtered and cracked noisily. Then Bob proposed:

"A merry Christmas to us all, my dears. God bless us!"

Which all the family re-echoed.

"God bless us everyone!" said Tiny Tim, the last of all.

Now I told you that Mr. Scrooge had some disagreeable and wonderful dreams on Christmas eve, and so he had; and in one of them he dreamt that a Christmas spirit showed him his clerk's home; he saw them all gathered round the fire, and heard them drink his health, and Tiny Tim's song, and he took special note of Tiny Tim himself.

How Mr. Scrooge spent Christmas day we do not know. He may have remained in bed, having a cold, but on Christmas night he had more dreams, and in one of his dreams the spirit took him again to his clerk's poor home. The mother was doing some needlework, seated by the table, a tear dropped on it now and then, and she said, poor thing, that the work, which was black, hurt her eyes. The children sat, sad and silent, about the room, except Tiny Tim, who was not there. Upstairs the father, with his face hidden in his hands, sat beside a little bed, on which lay a tiny figure, white and still. "My little child, my pretty little child," he sobbed, as the tears fell through his fingers on to the floor. "Tiny Tim died because his father was too poor to give him what was necessary to make him well; *you* kept him poor;" said the dream-spirit to Mr. Scrooge. The father kissed the cold, little face on the bed, and went downstairs, where the sprays of holly still remained about the humble room; and taking his hat, went out, with a wistful glance at the little crutch in the corner as he shut the door. Mr. Scrooge saw all this, and many more things as strange and sad, the spirit took care of that; but, wonderful to relate, he woke the next morning feeling a different man—feeling as he had never felt in his life before. For after all, you know that what he had seen was no more than a dream; he knew that Tiny Tim was not dead, and Scrooge was resolved that Tiny Tim should not die if he could help it.

"Why, I am as light as a feather, and as happy as an angel, and as merry as a schoolboy," Scrooge said to himself as he skipped into the next room to breakfast and threw on all the coals at once, and put two lumps of sugar in his tea. "I hope everybody had a merry Christmas, and here's a happy New Year to all the world."

On that morning, the day after Christmas poor Bob Cratchit crept into the office a few minutes late, expecting to be roundly abused and scolded for it, but no such thing; his master was there with his back to a good fire, and actually smiling, and he shook hands with his clerk, telling him heartily he was going to raise his salary and asking quite affectionately after Tiny Tim! "And mind you make up a good fire in your room before you set to work, Bob," he said, as he closed his own door.

Bob could hardly believe his eyes and ears, but it was all true. Such doings as they had on New Year's day had never been seen before in the Cratchits' home, nor such a turkey as Mr. Scrooge sent them for dinner. Tiny Tim had his share too, for Tiny Tim did not die, not a bit of it. Mr. Scrooge was a second father to him from that day, he wanted for nothing, and grew up strong and hearty. Mr. Scrooge loved him, and well he might, for was it not Tiny Tim who had without knowing it, through the Christmas dream-spirit, touched his hard heart and caused him to become a good and happy man?

III

The Runaway Couple

THE Boots at the Holly Tree Inn was the young man named Cobbs, who blacked the shoes, and ran errands, and waited on the people at the inn; and this is the story that he told, one day.

"Supposing a young gentleman not eight years old was to run away with a fine young woman of seven, would you consider that a queer start? That there is a start as I—the Boots at the Holly Tree Inn—have seen with my own eyes; and I cleaned the shoes they ran away in, and they was so little that I couldn't get my hand into 'em.

"Master Harry Walmers' father, he lived at the Elms, away by Shooter's Hill, six or seven miles from London. He was uncommon proud of Master Harry, as he was his only child; but he didn't spoil him neither. He was a gentleman that had a will of his own, and an eye of his own, and that would be minded. Consequently, though he made quite a companion of the fine bright boy, still he kept the command over him, and the child *was* a child. I was under-gardener there at that time; and one morning Master Harry, he comes to me and says—

"'Cobbs, how should you spell Norah, if you was asked?' and then begun cutting it in print, all over the fence.

"He couldn't say he had taken particular notice of children before that; but really it was pretty to see them two mites a-going about the place together, deep in love. And the courage of the boy! Bless your soul, he'd have throwed off his little hat, and tucked up his little sleeves, and gone in at a lion, he would, if they had happened to meet one and she had been frightened of him. One day he stops along, with her, where Boots was hoeing weeds in the gravel, and says—speaking up, 'Cobbs,' he says, 'I like you.' 'Do you, sir? I'm proud to hear it.' 'Yes, I do, Cobbs. Why do I like you, do you think, Cobbs?' 'Don't know, Master Harry, I am sure.' 'Because Norah likes you, Cobbs.' 'Indeed, sir? That's very gratifying.' 'Gratifying, Cobbs?

It's better than millions of the brightest diamonds to be liked by Norah.' 'Certainly, sir.' 'You're going away, ain't you, Cobbs?' 'Yes, sir.' 'Would you like another situation, Cobbs?' 'Well, sir, I shouldn't object, if it was a good 'un.' 'Then, Cobbs,' says he, 'you shall be our head-gardener when we are married.' And he tucks her, in her little sky-blue mantle, under his arm, and walks away.

"It was better than a picter, and equal to a play, to see them babies with their long, bright, curling hair, their sparkling eyes, and their beautiful light tread, a-rambling about the garden, deep in love. Boots was of opinion that the birds believed they was birds, and kept up with 'em, singing to please 'em. Sometimes, they would creep under the Tulip tree, and would sit there with their arms round one another's necks, and their soft cheeks touching, a-reading about the prince and the dragon, and the good and bad enchanters, and the king's fair daughter. Sometimes he would hear them planning about having a house in a forest, keeping bees and a cow, and living entirely on milk and honey. Once he came upon them by the pond, and heard Master Harry say, 'Adorable Norah, kiss me, and say you love me to distraction, or I'll jump in headforemost.' And Boots made no question he would have done it, if she hadn't done as he asked her.

"'Cobbs,' says Master Harry, one evening, when Cobbs was watering the flowers, 'I am going on a visit, this present mid-summer, to my grandmamma's at York.'

"'Are you, indeed, sir? I hope you'll have a pleasant time. I am going into Yorkshire myself when I leave here.'

"'Are you going to your grandmamma's, Cobbs?'

"'No, sir. I haven't got such a thing.'

"'Not as a grandmamma, Cobbs?'

"'No, sir.'

"The boy looked on at the watering of the flowers for a little while and then said, 'I shall be very glad, indeed, to go, Cobbs—Norah's going.'

"'You'll be all right then, sir,' says Cobbs, 'with your beautiful sweetheart by your side.'

"'Cobbs,' returned the boy, flushing, 'I never let anybody joke about it when I can prevent them.'

"'It wasn't a joke, sir,' says Cobbs, with humility—'wasn't so meant.'

"'I am glad of that, Cobbs, because I like you! you know, and you're going to live with us, Cobbs.

"'Sir.'

"'What do you think my grandmamma gives me, when I go down there?'

"'I couldn't so much as make a guess, sir.'

"'A Bank of England five-pound note, Cobbs.'[1]

"'Whew!' says Cobbs, 'that's a spanking sum of money, Master Harry.'

"'A person could do a great deal with such a sum of money as that. Couldn't a person, Cobbs?'

"'I believe you, sir!'

"'Cobbs,' said the boy, 'I'll tell you a secret. At Norah's house they have been joking her about me, and pretending to laugh at our being engaged. Pretending to make game of it, Cobbs!'

"'Such, sir,' says Cobbs, 'is the wickedness of human natur'.'

"The boy, looking exactly like his father, stood for a few minutes with his glowing face towards the sunset, and then departed with, 'Good night, Cobbs. I'm going in.'

"I was the Boots at the Holly Tree Inn when one summer afternoon the coach drives up, and out of the coach gets these two children.

"The guard says to our governor, the inn-keeper, 'I don't quite make out these little passengers, but the young gentleman's words was, that they were to be brought here.' The young gentleman gets

---

1. For the benefit of some of our young readers, it may be well to explain that this is about the same as a bill of twenty-five dollars would be in America.

out; hands his lady out; gives the driver something for himself; says to our governor, 'We're to stop here to-night, please. Sitting-room and two bedrooms will be required. Chops and cherry-pudding for two!' and tucks her, in her little sky-blue mantle, under his arm, and walks into the house much bolder than brass.

"Boots leaves me to judge what the amazement of that establishment was when those two tiny creatures, all alone by themselves, was marched into the parlor—much more so when he, who had seen them without their seeing him, gave the governor his views of the errand they was upon. 'Cobbs,' says the governor, 'if this is so, I must set off myself to York and quiet their friends' minds. In which case you must keep your eye upon 'em, and humor 'em, till I come back. But, before I take these measures, Cobbs, I should wish you to find out from themselves whether your opinions is correct.' 'Sir, to you,' says Cobbs, 'that shall be done directly.'

"So Boots goes up stairs to the parlor, and there he finds Master Harry on an enormous sofa a-drying the eyes of Miss Norah with his pocket-hankecher. Their little legs were entirely off the ground of course, and it really is not possible for Boots to express to me how small them children looked.

"'It's Cobbs! It's Cobbs!' cries Master Harry, and comes running to him, and catching hold of his hand. Miss Norah comes running to him on t'other side, and catching hold of his t'other hand, and they both jump for joy.

"'I see you a-getting out, sir,' says Cobbs. 'I thought it was you. I thought I couldn't be mistaken in your height and figure. What's the object of your journey, sir? Are you going to be married?'

"'We are going to be married, Cobbs, at Gretna Green,' returned the boy. 'We have run away on purpose. Norah has been in rather low spirits, Cobbs; but she'll be happy, now we have found you to be our friend.'

"'Thank you, sir, and thank *you*, miss,' says Cobbs, 'for your good opinion. Did you bring any luggage with you, sir?'

"If I will believe Boots when he gives me his word and honor upon it, the lady had got a parasol, a smelling-bottle, a round and a half of cold buttered toast, eight peppermint drops, and a hair-brush—seemingly a doll's. The gentleman had got about half a dozen yards of string, a knife, three or four sheets of writing-paper folded up surprisingly small, an orange, and a china mug with his name upon it.

"'What may be the exact natur' of your plans, sir?' says Cobbs.

"'To go on,' replied the boy—which the courage of that boy was something wonderful!—'in the morning, and be married to-morrow.'

"'Just so, sir,' says Cobbs. 'Would it meet your views, sir, if I was to go with you?'

"When Cobbs said this, they both jumped for joy again, and cried out, 'Oh, yes, yes, Cobbs! Yes!'

"'Well, sir,' says Cobbs. 'If you will excuse my having the freedom to give an opinion, what I should recommend would be this. I'm acquainted with a pony, sir, which, put in a phaeton that I could borrow, would take you and Mrs. Harry Walmers, Jr. (myself driving, if you agree), to the end of your journey in a very short space of time. I am not altogether sure, sir, that this pony will be at liberty to-morrow, but even if you had to wait over to-morrow for him, it might be worth your while. As to the small account for your board here, sir, in case you was to find yourself running at all short, that don't signify, because I'm a part proprietor of this inn, and it could stand over.'

"Boots tells me that when they clapped their hands and jumped for joy again, and called him, 'Good Cobbs!' and 'Dear Cobbs!' and bent across him to kiss one another in the delight of their trusting hearts, he felt himself the meanest rascal for deceiving 'em that ever was born.

"'Is there anything you want just at present, sir?' says Cobbs, mortally ashamed of himself.

"'We would like some cakes after dinner,' answered Master Harry, folding his arms, putting out one leg, and looking straight at him, 'and two apples—and jam. With dinner, we should like to have toast and water. But Norah has always been accustomed to half a glass of currant wine at dessert. And so have I.'

"'It shall be ordered at the bar, sir,' says Cobbs, and away he went.

"'The way in which the women of that house—without exception—everyone of 'em—married and single, took to that boy when they heard the story, Boots considers surprising. It was as much as he could do to keep 'em from dashing into the room and kissing him. They climbed up all sorts of places, at the risk of their lives, to look at him through a pane of glass. They were seven deep at the key-hole. They were out of their minds about him and his bold spirit.

"In the evening Boots went into the room, to see how the runaway couple was getting on. The gentleman was on the window-seat, supporting the lady in his arms. She had tears upon her face, and was lying, very tired and half-asleep, with her head upon his shoulder.

"'Mrs. Harry Walmers, Jr., tired, sir?' says Cobbs.

"'Yes, she is tired, Cobbs; but she is not used to be away from home, and she has been in low spirits again. Cobbs, do you think you could bring a biffin, please?'

"'I ask your pardon, sir,' says Cobbs. 'What was it you—'

"'I think a Norfolk biffin[2] would rouse her, Cobbs. She is very fond of them.'

"Boots withdrew in search of the required restorative, and, when he brought it in, the gentleman handed it to the lady, and fed her with a spoon, and took a little himself. The lady being heavy with sleep, and rather cross. 'What should you think, sir,' says Cobbs, 'of a chamber candlestick?' The gentleman approved; the chambermaid went first, up the great staircase; the lady, in her sky-blue mantle, followed, gallantly led by the gentleman; the gentleman kissed her at the door, and retired to his own room, where Boots softly locked him up.

"Boots couldn't but feel what a base deceiver he was when they asked him at breakfast (they had ordered sweet milk-and-water, and toast and currant jelly, overnight) about the pony. It really was as much as he could do, he don't mind confessing to me, to look them

2. A biffin is a red apple, growing near Norfolk, and generally eaten after having been baked.

two young things in the face, and think how wicked he had grown up to be. Howsomever, he went on a-lying like a Trojan, about the pony. He told 'em it did so unfortunately happen that the pony was half-clipped, you see, and that he couldn't be taken out in that state for fear that it should strike to his inside. But that he'd be finished clipping in the course of the day, and that to-morrow morning at eight o'clock the phaeton would be ready. Boots' view of the whole case, looking back upon it in my room, is, that Mrs. Harry Walmers, Jr., was beginning to give in. She hadn't had her hair curled when she went to bed, and she didn't seem quite up to brushing it herself, and it's getting in her eyes put her out. But nothing put out Master Harry. He sat behind his breakfast cup, a-tearing away at the jelly, as if he had been his own father.

"After breakfast Boots is inclined to think that they drawed soldiers—at least, he knows that many such was found in the fireplace, all on horseback. In the course of the morning Master Harry rang the bell—it was surprising how that there boy did carry on—and said in a sprightly way, 'Cobbs, is there any good walks in this neighborhood?'

"'Yes, sir,' says Cobbs. 'There's Love Lane.'

"'Get out with you, Cobbs!'—that was that there boy's expression—'you're joking.'

"'Begging your pardon, sir,' says Cobbs, 'there really is Love Lane. And a pleasant walk it is, and proud I shall be to show it to yourself and Mrs. Harry Walmers, Jr.'

"'Norah, dear,' said Master Harry, 'this is curious. We really ought to see Love Lane. Put on your bonnet, my sweetest darling, and we will go there with Cobbs.'

"Boots leaves me to judge what a beast he felt himself to be, when that young pair told him, as they all three jogged along together, that they had made up their minds to give him two thousand guineas a year as head-gardener, on account of his being so true a friend to 'em. Boots could have wished at the moment that the earth would have opened and swallowed him up; he felt so mean with their beaming eyes a-looking at him, and believing him. Well, sir, he turned the conversation as well as he could, and he took 'em down Love Lane to the water-meadows, and there Master Harry would have drowned himself in half a moment more, a-getting out a water-lily for her—but nothing frightened that boy. Well, sir, they was tired out. All being so new and strange to 'em, they was tired as tired could be. And they laid down on a bank of daisies, like the children in the wood, leastways meadows, and fell asleep.

"Well, sir, they woke up at last, and then one thing was getting pretty clear to Boots, namely, that Mrs. Harry Walmers', Jr., temper was on the move. When Master Harry took her round the waist she said he 'teased her so,' and when he says, 'Norah, my young May Moon, your Harry tease you?' she tells him, 'Yes; and I want to go home!'

"However, Master Harry he kept up, and his noble heart was as fond as ever. Mrs. Walmers turned very sleepy about dusk and began to cry. Therefore, Mrs. Walmers went off to bed as per yesterday; and Master Harry ditto repeated.

"About eleven or twelve at night comes back the inn-keeper in a chaise, along with Mr. Walmers and an elderly lady. Mr. Walmers looks amused and very serious, both at once, and says to our missis, 'We are very much indebted to you, ma'am, for your kind care of our little children, which we can never sufficiently acknowledge. Pray, ma'am where is my boy?' Our missis says, 'Cobbs has the dear children in charge, sir. Cobbs, show forty!' Then he says to Cobbs, 'Ah, Cobbs! I am glad to see *you*. I understand you was here!' And Cobbs says, 'Yes, sir. Your most obedient, sir.'

"I may be surprised to hear Boots say it, perhaps, but Boots assures me that his heart beat like a hammer, going up-stairs. 'I beg your pardon, sir,' says he, while unlocking the door; 'I hope you are not angry with Master Harry. For Master Harry is a fine boy, sir, and will do you credit and honor.' And Boots signifies to me that if the fine boy's father had contradicted him in the daring state of mind in which he then was, he thinks he should have 'fetched him a crack,' and taken the consequences.

"But Mr. Walmers only says, 'No, Cobbs. No, my good fellow. Thank you!' And the door being open, goes in.

"Boots goes in too, holding the light, and he sees Mr. Walmers go up to the bedside, bend gently down, and kiss the little sleeping face. Then he stands looking at it for a minute, looking wonderfully like it; and then he gently shakes the little shoulder.

"'Harry, my dear boy! Harry!'

"Master Harry starts up and looks at him. Looks at Cobbs, too. Such is the honor of that mite that he looks at Cobbs to see whether he has brought him into trouble.

"'I am not angry, my child. I only want you to dress yourself and come home.'

"'Yes, pa.'

"Master Harry dresses himself quickly. His breast begins to swell when he has nearly finished, and it swells more and more as he stands a-looking at his father; his father standing a-looking at him, the quiet image of him.

"'Please may I'—the spirit of that little creatur', and the way he kept his rising tears down!—'Please, dear pa—may I—kiss Norah before I go?'

"'You may, my child.'

"So he takes Master Harry in his hand, and Boots leads the way with the candle, and they come to that other bedroom; where the elderly lady is seated by the bed, and poor little Mrs. Harry Walmers, Jr., is fast asleep. There the father lifts the child up to the pillow, and he lays his little face down for an instant by the little warm face of poor unconscious little Mrs. Harry Walmers, Jr., and gently draws it to him—a sight so touching to the chambermaids who are peeping through the door that one of them calls out, 'It's a shame to part 'em!' But this chambermaid was always, as Boots informs me, a soft-hearted one. Not that there was any harm in that girl. Far from it."

IV

Little Dorrit

MANY years ago, when people could be put in prison for debt, a poor gentleman, who was unfortunate enough to lose all his money, was brought to the Marshalsea prison, which was the prison where debtors were kept. As there seemed no prospect of being able to pay his debts, his wife and their two little children came to live there with him. The elder child was a boy of three; the younger a little girl of two years old, and not long afterwards another little girl was born. The three children played in the courtyard, and on the whole were happy, for they were too young to remember a happier state of things.

But the youngest child, who had never been outside the prison walls, was a thoughtful little creature, and wondered what the outside world could be like. Her great friend, the turnkey, who was also her godfather, became very fond of her, and as soon as she could walk and talk he brought a little arm-chair and stood it by his fire at the lodge, and coaxed her with cheap toys to come and sit with him. In return the child loved him dearly, and would often bring her doll to dress and undress as she sat in the little arm-chair. She was still a very tiny creature when she began to understand that everyone did not live locked up inside high walls with spikes at the top, and though she and the rest of the family might pass through the door that the great key opened, her father could not; and she would look at him with a wondering pity in her tender little heart.

One day, she was sitting in the lodge gazing wistfully up at the sky through the barred window. The turnkey, after watching her some time, said:

"Thinking of the fields, ain't you?"

"Where are they?" she asked.

"Why, they're—over there, my dear," said the turnkey, waving his key vaguely, "just about there."

"Does anybody open them and shut them? Are they locked?"

"Well," said the turnkey, not knowing what to say, "not in general."

"Are they pretty, Bob?" She called him Bob, because he wished it.

"Lovely. Full of flowers. There's buttercups, and there's daisies, and there's—" here he hesitated not knowing the names of many flowers—"there's dandelions, and all manner of games."

"Is it very pleasant to be there, Bob?"

"Prime," said the turnkey.

"Was father ever there?"

"Hem!" coughed the turnkey. "O yes, he was there, sometimes."

"Is he sorry not to be there now?"

"N—not particular," said the turnkey.

"Nor any of the people?" she asked, glancing at the listless crowd within. "O are you quite sure and certain, Bob?"

At this point, Bob gave in and changed the subject to candy. But after this chat, the turnkey and little Amy would go out on his free Sunday afternoons to some meadows or green lanes, and she would pick grass and flowers to bring home, while he smoked his pipe; and then they would go to some tea-gardens for shrimps and tea and other delicacies, and would come back hand in hand, unless she was very tired and had fallen asleep on his shoulder.

When Amy was only eight years old, her mother died; and the poor father was more helpless and broken-down than ever, and as Fanny was a careless child and Edward idle, the little one, who had the bravest and truest heart, was led by her love and unselfishness to be the little mother of the forlorn family, and struggled to get some little education for herself and her brother and sister.

At first, such a baby could do little more than sit with her father, deserting her livelier place by the high fender, and quietly watching him. But this made her so far necessary to him that he became accustomed to her, and began to be sensible of missing her when she was not there. Through this little gate, she passed out of her childhood into the care-laden world.

What her pitiful look saw, at that early time, in her father, in her sister, in her brother, in the jail; how much or how little of the wretched truth it pleased God to make plain to her, lies hidden with many mysteries. It is enough that she was inspired to be something which was not what the rest were, and to be that something, different and laborious, for the sake of the rest. Inspired? Yes. Shall we speak of a poet or a priest, and not of the heart impelled by love and self-devotion to the lowliest work in the lowliest way of life?

The family stayed so long in the prison that the old man came to be known as "The Father of the Marshalsea;" and little Amy, who had never known any other home, as "The Child of the Marshalsea."

At thirteen she could read and keep accounts—that is, could put down in words and figures how much the bare necessaries that they wanted would cost, and how much less they had to buy them with. She had been, by snatches of a few weeks at a time, to an evening school outside, and got her sister and brother sent to day-schools from time to time during three or four years. There was no teaching for any of them at home; but she knew well—no one better—that a man so broken as to be the Father of the Marshalsea, could be no father to his own children.

To these scanty means of improvement, she added another of her own contriving. Once among the crowd of prisoners there appeared a dancing-master. Her sister had a great desire to learn the dancing-master's art, and seemed to have a taste that way. At thirteen years old, the Child of the Marshalsea presented herself to the dancing-master, with a little bag in her hand, and offered her humble petition.

"If you please, I was born here, sir."

"Oh! you are the young lady, are you?" said the dancing-master, surveying the small figure and uplifted face.

"Yes, sir."

"And what can I do for you?" said the dancing-master.

"Nothing for me, sir, thank you," anxiously undrawing the strings of the little bag; "but if, while you stay here, you could be so kind as to teach my sister cheap——"

"My child, I'll teach her for nothing," said the dancing-master, shutting up the bag. He was as good-natured a dancing-master as ever danced to the Insolvent Court, and he kept his word. The sister was so apt a pupil, and the dancing-master had such abundant time to give her, that wonderful progress was made. Indeed, the dancing-master was so proud of it, and so wishful to show it before he left, to a few select friends among the collegians (the debtors in the prison were called "collegians"), that at six o'clock on a certain fine morning, an exhibition was held in the yard—the college-rooms being of too small size for the purpose—in which so much ground was covered, and the steps were so well executed, that the dancing-master, having to play his fiddle besides, was thoroughly tired out.

The success of this beginning, which led to the dancing-master's continuing his teaching after his release, led the poor child to try again. She watched and waited months for a seamstress. In the fullness of time a milliner came in, sent there like all the rest for a debt which she could not pay; and to her she went to ask a favor for herself.

"I beg your pardon, ma'am," she said, looking timidly round the door of the milliner, whom she found in tears and in bed: "but I was born here."

Everybody seemed to hear of her as soon as they arrived; for the milliner sat up in bed, drying her eyes, and said, just as the dancing-master had said:

"Oh! *you* are the child, are you?"

"Yes, ma'am."

"I am sorry I haven't got anything for you," said the milliner, shaking her head.

"It's not that, ma'am. If you please, I want to learn needlework."

"Why should you do that," returned the milliner, "with me before you? It has not done me much good."

"Nothing—whatever it is—seems to have done anybody much good who comes here," she returned in her simple way; "but I want to learn, just the same."

"I am afraid you are so weak, you see," the milliner objected.

"I don't think I am weak, ma'am."

"And you are so very, very little, you see," the milliner objected.

"Yes, I am afraid I am very little indeed," returned the Child of the Marshalsea; and so began to sob over that unfortunate smallness of hers, which came so often in her way. The milliner—who was not unkind or hardhearted, only badly in debt—was touched, took her in hand with good-will, found her the most patient and earnest of pupils, and made her a good workwoman.

In course of time, the Father of the Marshalsea gradually developed a new trait of character. He was very greatly ashamed of having his two daughters work for their living; and tried to make it appear that they were only doing work for pleasure, not for pay. But at the same time he would take money from any one who would give it to him, without any sense of shame. With the same hand that had pocketed a fellow-prisoner's half-crown half an hour ago, he would wipe away the tears that streamed over his cheeks if anything was spoken of his daughters' earning their bread. So, over and above her other daily cares, the Child of the Marshalsea had always upon her the care of keeping up the make-believe that they were all idle beggars together.

The sister became a dancer. There was a ruined uncle in the family group—ruined by his brother, the Father of the Marshalsea, and knowing no more how, than his ruiner did, but taking the fact as something that could not be helped. Naturally a retired and simple man, he had shown no particular sense of being ruined, at the time when that calamity fell upon him, further than he left off washing himself when the shock was announced, and never took to washing his face and hands any more. He had been a rather poor musician in his better days; and when he fell with his brother, supported himself in a poor way by playing a clarionet as dirty as himself in a small theatre band. It was the theatre in which his niece became a dancer; he had been a fixture there a long time when she took her poor station in it; and he accepted the task of serving as her guardian, just as he would have accepted an illness, a legacy, a feast, starvation—anything but soap.

To enable this girl to earn her few weekly shillings, it was necessary for the Child of the Marshalsea to go through a careful form with her father.

"Fanny is not going to live with us, just now, father. She will be here a good deal in the day, but she is going to live outside with uncle."

"You surprise me. Why?"

"I think uncle wants a companion, father. He should be attended to and looked after."

"A companion? He passes much of his time here. And you attend and look after him, Amy, a great deal more than ever your sister will. You all go out so much; you all go out so much."

This was to keep up the form and pretense of his having no idea that Amy herself went out by the day to work.

"But we are always very glad to come home father; now, are we not? And as to Fanny, perhaps besides keeping uncle company and taking care of him, it may be as well for her not quite to live here always. She was not born here as I was you know, father."

"Well, Amy, well. I don't quite follow you, but it's natural I suppose that Fanny should prefer to be outside, and even that you often should, too. So, you and Fanny and your uncle, my dear, shall have your own way. Good, good. I'll not meddle; don't mind me."

To get her brother out of the prison; out of the low work of running errands for the prisoners outside, and out of the bad company into which he had fallen, was her hardest task. At eighteen years of age her brother Edward would have dragged on from hand to mouth, from hour to hour, from penny to penny, until eighty. Nobody got into the prison from whom he gained anything useful or good, and she could find no patron for him but her old friend and godfather, the turnkey.

"Dear Bob," said she, "what is to become of poor Tip?" His name was Edward, and Ted had been changed into Tip, within the walls.

The turnkey had strong opinions of his own as to what would become of poor Tip, and had even gone so far with the view of preventing their fulfilment, as to talk to Tip in urging him to run away and serve his country as a soldier. But Tip had thanked him, and said he didn't seem to care for his country.

"Well, my dear," said the turnkey, "something ought to be done with him. Suppose I try and get him into the law?"

"That would be so good of you, Bob!"

The turnkey now began to speak to the lawyers as they passed in and out of the prison. He spoke so perseveringly that a stool and twelve shillings a week were at last found for Tip in the office of a lawyer at Clifford's Inn, in the Palace Court.

Tip idled in Clifford's Inn for six months, and at the end of that term sauntered back one evening with his hands in his pockets, and remarked to his sister that he was not going back again.

"Not going back again?" said the poor little anxious Child of the Marshalsea, always calculating and planning for Tip, in the front rank of her charges.

"I am so tired of it," said Tip, "that I have cut it."

Tip tired of everything. With intervals of Marshalsea lounging, and errand-running, his small second mother, aided by her trusty friend, got him into a warehouse, into a market garden, into the hop trade, into the law again, into an auctioneer's, into a brewery, into a stockbroker's, into the law again, into a coach office, into a wagon office, into the law again, into a general dealer's, into a distillery, into the law again, into a wool house, into a dry goods house, into the fish-market, into the foreign fruit trade, and into the docks. But whatever Tip went into he came out of tired, announcing that he had cut it. Wherever he went, this useless Tip appeared to take the prison walls with him, and to set them up in such trade or calling; and to prowl about within their narrow limits in the old slipshod, purposeless, down-at-heel way; until the real immovable Marshalsea walls asserted their power over him and brought him back.

Nevertheless, the brave little creature did so fix her heart on her brother's rescue that, while he was ringing out these doleful changes, she pinched and scraped enough together to ship him for Canada. When he was tired of nothing to do, and disposed in its turn to cut even that, he graciously consented to go to Canada. And there was grief in her bosom over parting with him, and joy in the hope of his being put in a straight course at last.

"God bless you, dear Tip. Don't be too proud to come and see us, when you have made your fortune."

"All right!" said Tip, and went.

But not all the way to Canada; in fact, not further than Liverpool. After making the voyage to that port from London, he found himself so strongly impelled to cut the vessel, that he resolved to walk back again. Carrying out which intention, he presented himself before her at the expiration of a month, in rags, without shoes, and much more tired than ever.

At length, after another period of running errands, he found a pursuit for himself, and announced it.

"Amy, I have got a situation."

"Have you really and truly, Tip?"

"All right. I shall do now. You needn't look anxious about me any more, old girl."

"What is it, Tip?"

"Why, you know Slingo by sight?"

"Not the man they call the dealer?"

"That's the chap. He'll be out on Monday, and he's going to give me a berth."

"What is he a dealer in, Tip?"

"Horses. All right! I shall do now, Amy."

She lost sight of him for months afterwards, and only heard from him once. A whisper passed among the elder prisoners that he had been seen at a mock auction in Moorfields, pretending to buy plated articles for real silver, and paying for them with the greatest liberality in bank-notes; but it never reached her ears. One evening she was alone at work—standing up at the window, to save the twilight lingering above the wall—when he opened the door and walked in.

She kissed and welcomed him; but was afraid to ask him any question. He saw how anxious and timid she was, and appeared sorry.

"I am afraid, Amy, you'll be vexed this time. Upon my life I am!"

"I am very sorry to hear you say so, Tip. Have you come back?"

"Why—yes."

"Not expecting this time that what you had found would answer very well, I am less surprised and sorry than I might have been, Tip."

"Ah! But that's not the worst of it."

"Not the worst of it?"

"Don't look so startled. No, Amy, not the worst of it. I have come back, you see; but—*don't* look so startled—I have come back in what I may call a new way. I am off the volunteer list altogether. I am in now, as one of the regulars. I'm here in prison for debt, like everybody else."

"Oh! Don't say that you are a prisoner, Tip! Don't, don't!"

"Well, I don't want to say it," he returned in unwilling tone; "but if you can't understand me without my saying it, what am I to do? I am in for forty pound odd."

For the first time in all those years, she sunk under her cares. She cried, with her clasped hands lifted above her head, that it would kill their father if he ever knew it; and fell down at Tip's worthless feet.

It was easier for Tip to bring her to her senses than for her to bring *him* to understand that the Father of the Marshalsea would be beside himself if he knew the truth. Tip thought that there was nothing strange in being there a prisoner, but he agreed that his father should not be told about it. There were plenty of reasons that could be given for his return; it was accounted for to the father in the usual way; and the collegians, with a better understanding of the kind fraud than Tip, stood by it faithfully.

This was the life, and this the history, of the Child of the Marshalsea, at twenty-two. With a still abiding interest in the one miserable yard and block of houses as her birthplace and home, she passed to and fro in it shrinking now, with a womanly consciousness that she was pointed out to everyone. Since she had begun to work beyond the walls, she had found it necessary to hide where she lived, and to come and go secretly as she could, between the free city and the iron gates, outside of which she had never slept in her life. Her original timidity had grown with this concealment, and her light step and her little figure shunned the thronged streets while they passed along them.

"Mr. Clennam Followed Her Home."

Worldly wise in hard and poor necessities, she was innocent in all things else. Innocent, in the mist through which she saw her father, and the prison, and the dark living river that flowed through it and flowed on.

This was the life, and this the history, of Little Dorrit, until the son of a lady, Mrs. Clennam, to whose house Amy went to do needlework, became interested in the pale, patient little creature. He followed her to her home one day and when he found that it was the debtor's prison, he walked in. Learning her sad history from her father, Arthur Clennam resolved to do his best to try to get him released and to help them all.

One day when he was walking home with Amy to try to find out the names of some of the people her father owed money to, a voice was heard calling, "Little mother, little mother," and a strange figure came bouncing up to them and fell down, scattering her basketful of potatoes on the ground. "Oh Maggie," said Amy, "what a clumsy child you are!"

She was about eight and twenty, with large bones, large features, large hands and feet, large eyes, and no hair. Amy told Mr. Clennam that Maggie was the granddaughter of her old nurse, who had been dead a long time, and that her grandmother had been very unkind to her and beat her.

"When Maggie was ten years old she had a fever, and she has never grown older since."

"Ten years old," said Maggie. "But what a nice hospital! So comfortable, wasn't it? Such a 'e'v'nly place! Such beds there is there! Such lemonades! Such oranges! Such delicious broth and wine! Such chicking! Oh, AIN'T it a delightful place to stop at!"

"Poor Maggie thought that a hospital was the nicest place in all the world, because she had never seen another home as good. For years and years she looked back to the hospital as a sort of heaven on earth."

"Then when she came out, her grandmother did not know what to do with her, and was very unkind. But after some time Maggie tried to improve, and was very attentive and industrious and now she can earn her own living entirely, sir!"

Amy did not say who had taken pains to teach and encourage the poor half-witted creature, but Mr. Clennam guessed from the name "little mother" and the fondness of the poor creature for Amy.

One cold, wet evening, Amy and Maggie went to Mr. Clennam's house to thank him for having freed Edward from the prison, and on coming out found it was too late to get home, as the gate was locked. They tried to get in at Maggie's lodgings, but, though they knocked twice, the people were asleep. As Amy did not wish to disturb them, they wandered about all night, sometimes sitting at the gate of the prison, Maggie shivering and whimpering.

"It will soon be over, dear," said patient Amy.

"Oh, it's all very well for you, mother," said Maggie, "but I'm a poor thing, only ten years old."

Thanks to Mr. Clennam, a great change took place in the fortunes of the family, and not long after this wretched night it was discovered that Mr. Dorrit was owner of a large property, and they became very rich.

But Little Dorrit never forgot, as, sad to say, the rest of the family did, the friends who had been kind to them in their poverty; and when, in his turn, Mr. Clennam became a prisoner in the Marshalsea, Little Dorrit came to comfort and console him, and after many changes of fortune she became his wife, and they lived happy ever after.

V

The Toy-Maker and his Blind Daughter

CALEB PLUMMER and his blind daughter lived alone in a little cracked nutshell of a house. They were toy-makers, and their house, which was so small that it might have been knocked to pieces with a hammer, and carried away in a cart, was stuck like a toadstool on to the premises of Messrs. Gruff & Tackleton, the toy merchants for whom they worked—the latter of whom was himself both Gruff and Tackleton in one.

I am saying that Caleb and his blind daughter lived here. I should say Caleb did, while his daughter lived in an enchanted palace, which her father's love had created for her. She did not know that the ceilings were cracked, the plaster tumbling down, and the woodwork rotten; that everything was old and ugly and poverty-stricken about her, and that her father was a gray-haired, stooping old man, and the master for whom they worked a hard and brutal taskmaster; oh, dear no, she fancied a pretty, cosy, compact little home full of tokens of a kind master's care, a smart, brisk, gallant-looking father, and a handsome and noble-looking toy merchant who was an angel of goodness.

This was all Caleb's doing. When his blind daughter was a baby he had determined, in his great love and pity for her, that her loss of sight should be turned into a blessing, and her life as happy as he could make it. And she was happy; everything about her she saw with her father's eyes, in the rainbow-colored light with which it was his care and pleasure to invest it.

Caleb and his daughter were at work together in their usual working-room, which served them for their ordinary living-room as well; and a strange place it was. There were houses in it, finished and unfinished, for dolls of all stations in life. Tenement houses for dolls of moderate means; kitchens and single apartments for dolls of the lower classes; capital town residences for dolls of high estate. Some of these establishments were already furnished with a view to the needs of dolls of little money; others could be fitted on the most expensive scale, at a moment's notice, from whole shelves of chairs and tables, sofas, bedsteads, and upholstery. The nobility and gentry and public in general, for whose use these doll-houses were planned, lay, here and there, in baskets, staring straight up at the ceiling; but in showing their degrees in society, and keeping them in their own stations (which is found to be exceedingly difficult in real life), the makers of these dolls had far improved on nature, for they, not resting on such marks as satin, cotton-print, and bits of rag, had made differences which allowed of no mistake. Thus, the doll-lady of high rank had wax limbs of perfect shape; but only she and those of her grade; the next grade in the social scale being made of leather; and the next coarse linen stuff. As to the common-people, they had just so many matches out of tinder-boxes for their arms and legs, and there they were—established in their place at once, beyond the possibility of getting out of it.

There were various other samples of his handicraft besides dolls in Caleb Plummer's room. There were Noah's Arks, in which the birds and beasts were an uncommonly tight fit, I assure you; though they could be crammed in, anyhow, at the roof, and rattled and shaken into the smallest compass. Most of these Noah's Arks had knockers on the doors; perhaps not exactly suitable to an Ark as suggestive of morning callers and a postman, yet a pleasant finish to the outside of the building. There were scores of melancholy little carts, which, when the wheels went round, performed most doleful music. Many small fiddles, drums, and other instruments of torture; no end of cannon, shields, swords, spears, and guns. There were little tumblers in red breeches, incessantly swarming up high obstacles of red-tape, and coming down, head first, upon the other side; and there were innumerable old gentlemen of respectable, even venerable, appearance, flying like crazy people over pegs, inserted, for the purpose, in their own street-doors. There were beasts of all sorts, horses, in particular, of every breed, from the spotted barrel on four pegs, with a small tippet for a mane, to the fine rocking horse on his highest mettle.

"You were out in the rain last night in your beautiful new overcoat," said Bertha.

"Yes, in my beautiful new overcoat," answered Caleb, glancing to where a roughly-made garment of sackcloth was hung up to dry.

"How glad I am you bought it, father."

"And of such a tailor! quite a fashionable tailor; a bright blue cloth, with bright buttons; it's a deal too good a coat for me."

"Too good!" cried the blind girl, stopping to laugh and clap her hands—"as if anything was too good for my handsome father, with his smiling face, and black hair, and his straight figure, as if *any* thing could be too good for my handsome father!"

"I'm half ashamed to wear it, though," said Caleb, watching the effect of what he said upon her brightening face; "upon my word. When I hear the boys and people say behind me: 'Halloa! Here's a swell!' I don't know which way to look. And when the beggar wouldn't go away last night; and, when I said I was a very common man, said 'No, your honor! Bless your honor, don't say that!' I was quite ashamed. I really felt as if I hadn't a right to wear it."

Happy blind girl! How merry she was in her joy!

"I see you, father," she said, clasping her hands, "as plainly as if I had the eyes I never want when you are with me. A blue coat!"——

"Bright blue," said Caleb.

"Yes, yes! Bright blue!" exclaimed the girl, turning up her radiant face; "the color I can just remember in the blessed sky! You told me it was blue before! A bright blue coat——"

"Made loose to the figure," suggested Caleb.

"Yes! loose to the figure!" cried the blind girl, laughing heartily; "and in it you, dear father, with your merry eye, your smiling face, your free step, and your dark hair; looking so young and handsome!"

"Halloa! Halloa!" said Caleb. "I shall be vain presently."

"I think you are already," cried the blind girl, pointing at him, in her glee. "I know you, father! Ha, ha, ha! I've found you out, you see!"

How different the picture in her mind from Caleb, as he sat observing her! She had spoken of his free step. She was right in that. For years and years he never once had crossed that threshold at his own slow pace, but with a footfall made ready for her ear, and never had he, when his heart was heaviest, forgotten the light tread that was to render hers so cheerful and courageous.

"There we are," said Caleb, falling back a pace or two to form the better judgment of his work; "as near the real thing as sixpen'orth of halfpence is to sixpence. What a pity that the whole front of the house opens at once! If there was only a staircase in it now, and regular doors to the rooms to go in at! but that's the worst of my calling. I'm always fooling myself, and cheating myself."

"You are speaking quite softly. You are not tired, father?"

"Tired," echoed Caleb, with a great burst in his manner, "what should tire me, Bertha? *I* was never tired. What does it mean?"

To give the greater force to his words, he stopped himself in an imitation of two small stretching and yawning figures on the mantel-shelf, who were shown as in one eternal state of weariness from the waist upwards; and hummed a bit of a song. It was a drinking song, something about a sparkling bowl; and he sang it with an air of a devil-may-care voice, that made his face a thousand times more meager and more thoughtful than ever.

"What! you're singing, are you?" said Tackleton, the toy-seller for whom he worked, putting his head in at the door. "Go it! *I* can't sing."

Nobody would have thought that Tackleton *could* sing. He hadn't what is generally termed a singing face, by any means.

"I can't afford to sing," said Tackleton. "I'm glad you can. I hope you can afford to work, too. Hardly time for both, I should think?"

"If you could only see him, Bertha, how he's winking at me!" whispered Caleb. "Such a man to joke! you'd think, if you didn't know him, he was in earnest, wouldn't you, now?"

The blind girl smiled and nodded.

"I am thanking you for the little tree, the beautiful little tree," replied Bertha, bringing forward a tiny rose-tree in blossom, which, by an innocent story, Caleb had made her believe was her master's gift, though he himself had gone without a meal or two to buy it.

"The bird that can sing and won't sing must be made to sing, they say," grumbled Tackleton. "What about the owl that can't sing, and oughtn't to sing, and will sing; is there anything that he should be made to do?"

"The extent to which he's winking at this moment!" whispered Caleb to his daughter. "Oh, my gracious!"

"Always merry and light-hearted with us!" cried the smiling Bertha.

"Oh! you're there, are you?" answered Tackleton. "Poor idiot!"

He really did believe she was an idiot; and he founded the belief, I can't say whether consciously or not, upon her being fond of him.

"Well! and being there—how are you?" said Tackleton, in his cross way.

"Oh! well; quite well. And as happy as even you can wish me to be. As happy as you would make the whole world, if you could!"

"Poor idiot!" muttered Tackleton. "No gleam of reason! Not a gleam!"

The blind girl took his hand and kissed it; held it for a moment in her own two hands; and laid her cheek against it tenderly, before releasing it. There was such unspeakable affection and such fervent gratitude in the act, that Tackleton himself was moved to say, in a milder growl than usual:

"What's the matter now?"

"Bertha!" said Tackleton, assuming, for once, a little cordiality. "Come here."

"Oh! I can come straight to you. You needn't guide me," she rejoined.

"Shall I tell you a secret, Bertha?"

"If you will!" she answered, eagerly.

How bright the darkened face! How adorned with light the listening head!

"This is the day on which little what's-her-name, the spoilt child, Peerybingle's wife, pays her regular visit to you—makes her ridiculous picnic here; ain't it?" said Tackleton, with a strong expression of distaste for the whole concern.

"Yes," replied Bertha. "This is the day."

"I thought so!" said Tackleton. "I should like to join the party."

"Do you hear that, father!" cried the blind girl in delight.

"Yes, yes, I hear it," murmured Caleb, with the fixed look of a sleep-walker "but I do not believe it. It's one of my lies, I've no doubt."

"You see I—I want to bring the Peerybingles a little more into company with May Fielding," said Tackleton. "I am going to be married to May."

"Married!" cried the blind girl, starting from him.

"She's such a confounded idiot," muttered Tackleton, "that I was afraid she'd never understand me. Yes, Bertha! Married! Church, parson, clerk, glass-coach, bells, breakfast, bride-cake, favors, marrow-bones, cleavers, and all the rest of the tomfoolery. A wedding, you know; a wedding. Don't you know what a wedding is?"

"I know," replied the blind girl, in a gentle tone. "I understand!"

"Do you?" muttered Tackleton. "It's more than I expected. Well, on that account I want you to join the party, and to bring May and her mother. I'll send a little something or other, before the afternoon. A cold leg of mutton, or some comfortable trifle of that sort. You'll expect me?"

"Yes," she answered.

She had drooped her head, and turned away; and so stood, with her hands crossed, musing.

"I don't think you will," muttered Tackleton, looking at her; "for you seem to have forgotten all about it already. Caleb!"

"I may venture to say, I'm here, I suppose," thought Caleb. "Sir!"

"Take care she don't forget what I've been saying to her."

"*She* never forgets," returned Caleb. "It's one of the few things she ain't clever in."

"Every man thinks his own geese swans," observed the toy merchant, with a shrug. "Poor devil!"

Having delivered himself of which remark with infinite contempt, old Gruff & Tackleton withdrew.

Bertha remained where he had left her, lost in meditation. The gaiety had vanished from her downcast face, and it was very sad. Three or four times she shook her head, as if bewailing some remembrance or some loss; but her sorrowful reflections found no vent in words.

"Father, I am lonely in the dark. I want my eyes; my patient, willing eyes."

"Here they are," said Caleb. "Always ready. They are more yours than mine, Bertha, any hour in the four-and-twenty. What shall your eyes do for you, dear?"

"Look round the room, father."

"All right," said Caleb. "No sooner said than done, Bertha."

"Tell me about it."

"It's much the same as usual," said Caleb. "Homely, but very snug. The gay colors on the walls; the bright flowers on the plates and dishes; the shining wood, where there are beams or panels; the general cheerfulness and neatness of the building, make it very pretty."

Cheerful and neat it was, wherever Bertha's hands could busy themselves. But nowhere else were cheerfulness and neatness possible, in the crazy shed which Caleb's fancy so transformed.

"You have your working dress on, and are not so gay as when you wear the handsome coat?" said Bertha, touching him.

"Not quite so gay," answered Caleb. "Pretty brisk though."

"Father," said the blind girl, drawing close to his side and stealing one arm round his neck, "tell me something about May. She is very fair."

"She is, indeed," said Caleb. And she was indeed. It was quite a rare thing to Caleb not to have to draw on his invention.

"Her hair is dark," said Bertha, pensively, "darker than mine. Her voice is sweet and musical I know. I have often loved to hear it. Her shape—"

"There's not a doll's in all the room to equal it," said Caleb. "And her eyes—"

He stopped; for Bertha had drawn closer round his neck; and, from the arm that clung about him, came a warning pressure which he understood too well.

He coughed a moment, hammered for a moment, and then fell back upon the song about the sparkling bowl; the song which helped him through all such difficulties.

"Our friend, father; the one who has helped us so many times, Mr. Tackleton. I am never tired you know, of hearing about him. Now was I, ever?" she said, hastily.

"Of course not," answered Caleb. "And with reason."

"Ah! with how much reason?" cried the blind girl, with such fervency that Caleb, though his motives were pure, could not endure to meet her face, but dropped his eyes, as if she could have read in them his innocent deceit.

"Then tell me again about him, dear father," said Bertha. "Many times again! His face is good, kind, and tender. Honest and true, I am sure it is. The manly heart that tries to cloak all favors with a show of roughness and unwillingness beats in its every look and glance."

"And makes it noble," added Caleb in his quiet desperation.

"And makes it noble!" cried the blind girl. "He is older than May, father?"

"Ye-es," said Caleb, reluctantly. "He's a little older than May, but that don't signify."

"Bertha," said Caleb softly, "what has happened? How changed you are, my darling, in a few hours—since this morning. *You* silent and dull all day! What is it? Tell me!"

"Oh father, father!" cried the blind girl, bursting into tears. "Oh, my hard, hard fate!"

Caleb drew his hand across his eyes before he answered her.

"But think how cheerful and how happy you have been, Bertha! How good, and how much loved, by many people."

"That strikes me to the heart, dear father! Always so mindful of me! Always so kind to me!"

Caleb was very much perplexed to understand her.

"To be—to be blind, Bertha, my poor dear," he faltered, "is a great affliction; but——"

"I have never felt it!" cried the blind girl. "I have never felt it in its fullness. Never! I have sometimes wished that I could see you, or could see him; only once, dear father; only for one little minute. But, father! Oh, my good, gentle father, bear with me, if I am wicked!" said the blind girl. "This is not the sorrow that so weighs me down!"

"Bertha, my dear!" said Caleb, "I have something on my mind I want to tell you, while we are alone. Hear me kindly! I have a confession to make to you, my darling."

"A confession, father?"

"I have wandered from the truth and lost myself, my child," said Caleb, with a pitiable look on his bewildered face. "I have wandered from the truth, intending to be kind to you; and have been cruel."

She turned her wonder-stricken face towards him, and repeated, "Cruel! He cruel to me!" cried Bertha, with a smile of incredulity.

"Not meaning it, my child," said Caleb. "But I have been; though I never suspected it till yesterday. My dear blind daughter, hear me and forgive me! The world you live in, heart of mine, doesn't exist as I have represented it. The eyes you have trusted in have been false to you."

She turned her wonder-stricken face towards him still.

"Your road in life was rough, my poor one," said Caleb, "and I meant to smooth it for you. I have altered objects, invented many things that never have been, to make you happier. I have had concealments from you, put deceptions on you, God forgive me! and surrounded you with fancies."

"But living people are not fancies?" she said hurriedly, and turning very pale, and still retiring from him. "You can't change them."

"I have done so, Bertha," pleaded Caleb. "There is one person that you know, my Dove—"

"Oh, father! why do you say I know?" she answered in a tone of keen reproach. "What and whom do I know! I, who have no leader! I, so miserably blind!"

In the anguish of her heart she stretched out her hands, as if she were groping her way; then spread them, in a manner most forlorn and sad, upon her face.

"The marriage that takes place to-day," said Caleb, "is with a stern, sordid, grinding man. A hard master to you and me, my dear, for many years. Ugly in his looks and in his nature. Cold and callous always. Unlike what I have painted him to you in everything, my child. In everything."

"Oh, why," cried the blind girl, tortured, as it seemed, almost beyond endurance, "why did you ever do this? Why did you ever fill my heart so full, and then come in, like death, and tear away the objects of my love? Oh, heaven, how blind I am! How helpless and alone!"

Her afflicted father hung his head, and offered no reply but in his grief.

"Tell me what my home is. What it truly is."

"It is a poor place, Bertha; very poor and bare indeed. The house will scarcely keep out wind and rain another winter. It is as roughly shielded from the weather, Bertha, as your poor father in his sackcloth coat."

"Those presents that I took such care of, that came almost at my wish, and were so dearly welcome to me," she said, trembling; "where did they come from?"

Caleb did not answer. She knew already, and was silent.

"I see, I understand," said Bertha, "and now I am looking at you, at my kind, loving compassionate father, tell me what is he like?"

"An old man, my child; thin, bent, gray-haired, worn-out with hard work and sorrow; a weak, foolish, deceitful old man."

The blind girl threw herself on her knees before him, and took his gray head in her arms. "It is my sight, it is my sight restored," she cried. "I have been blind, but now I see; I have never till now truly seen my father. Does he think that there is a gay, handsome father in this earth that I could love so dearly, cherish so devotedly, as this worn and gray-headed old man? Father there is not a gray hair on your head that shall be forgotten in my prayers and thanks to heaven."

"My Bertha!" sobbed Caleb, "and the brisk smart father in the blue coat—he's gone, my child."

"Dearest father, no, he's not gone, nothing is gone, everything I loved and believed in is here in this worn, old father of mine, and more—oh, so much more, too! I have been happy and contented, but I shall be happier and more contented still, now that I know what you are. I am *not* blind, father, any longer."

VI

Little Nell

Little Nell and Her Grandfather

THE house where little Nell and her grandfather lived was one of those places where old and curious things were kept, one of those old houses which seem to crouch in odd corners of the town, and to hide their musty treasures from the public eye in jealousy and distrust. There were suits of mail standing like ghosts in armor, here and there; curious carvings brought from monkish cloisters; rusty weapons of various kinds; distorted figures in china, and wood, and iron, and ivory; tapestry, and strange furniture that might have been designed in dreams; and in the old, dark, dismal rooms there lived alone together the man and a child—his grandchild, Little Nell. Solitary and dull as was her life, the innocent and cheerful spirit of the child found happiness in all things, and through the dim rooms of the old curiosity shop Little Nell went singing, moving with gay and lightsome step.

But gradually over the old man, whom she so tenderly loved, there stole a sad change. He became thoughtful, sad and wretched. He had no sleep or rest but that which he took by day in his easy-chair; for every night, and all night long, he was away from home. To the child it seemed that her grandfather's love for her increased, even with the hidden grief by which she saw him struck down. And to see him sorrowful, and not to know the cause of his sorrow; to see him growing pale and weak under his trouble of mind, so weighed upon her gentle spirit that at times she felt as though her heart must break.

At last the time came when the old man's feeble frame could bear up no longer against his hidden care. A raging fever seized him, and, as he lay delirious or insensible through many weeks, Nell learned that the house which sheltered them was theirs no longer; that in the future they would be very poor; that they would scarcely have bread to eat. At length the old man began to mend, but his mind was weakened.

He would sit for hours together, with Nell's small hand in his, playing with the fingers, and sometimes stopping to smooth her hair or kiss her brow; and when he saw that tears were glistening in her eyes he would look amazed. As the time drew near when they must leave the house, he made no reference to the necessity of finding other shelter. An indistinct idea he had that the child was desolate and in need of help; though he seemed unable to understand their real position more distinctly. But a change came upon him one evening, as he and Nell sat silently together.

"Let us speak softly, Nell," he said. "Hush! for if they knew our purpose they would say that I was mad, and take thee from me. We will not stop here another day. We will travel afoot through the fields and woods, and trust ourselves to God in the places where He dwells. To-morrow morning, dear, we'll turn our faces from this scene of sorrow, and be as free and happy as the birds."

The child's heart beat high with hope and confidence. She had no thought of hunger, or cold, or thirst, or suffering. To her it seemed that they might beg their way from door to door in happiness, so that they were together.

When the day began to glimmer they stole out of the house, and, passing into the street, stood still.

"Which way?" asked the child.

The old man looked doubtfully and helplessly at her, and shook his head. It was plain that she was thenceforth his guide and leader. The child felt it, but had no doubts or misgivings, and, putting her hand in his, led him gently away. Forth from the city, while it yet was asleep went the two poor wanderers, going, they knew not whither.

They passed through the long, deserted streets, in the glad light of early morning, until these streets dwindled away, and the open country was about them. They walked all day, and slept that night at a small cottage where beds were let to travelers. The sun was setting on the second day of their journey, and they were jaded and worn out with walking, when, following a path which led through a churchyard to the town where they were to spend the night, they fell in with two traveling showmen, the exhibitors or keepers of a Punch and Judy show. These two men raised their eyes when the old man and his young companion were close upon them. One of them, the real exhibitor, no doubt, was a little, merry-faced man with a twinkling eye and a red nose, who seemed to be something like old Punch himself. The other—that was he who took the money—had rather a careful and cautious look, which perhaps came from his business also.

The merry man was the first to greet the strangers with a nod; and following the old man's eyes, he observed that perhaps that was the first time he had ever seen a Punch off the stage.

"Why do you come here to do this?" said the old man sitting down beside them, and looking at the figures with extreme delight.

"Why, you see," rejoined the little man, "we're putting up for to-night at the public house yonder, and it wouldn't do to let 'em see the present company undergoing repair."

"No!" cried the old man, making signs to Nell to listen, "why not, eh? why not?"

"Because it would destroy all the reality of the show and take away all the interest, wouldn't it?" replied the little man. "Would you care a ha'penny for the Lord Chancellor if you know'd him in private and without his wig?—certainly not."[3]

3.   The Lord Chancellor, it may be explained, is the highest judge in the courts of England; and when in court always wears a great wig and a robe.

"Good!" said the old man, venturing to touch one of the puppets, and drawing away his hand with a shrill laugh. "Are you going to show 'em to-night? are you?"

"That is the purpose, governor," replied the other, "and unless I'm much mistaken, Tommy Codlin is a-calculating at this minute what we've lost through your coming upon us. Cheer up, Tommy, it can't be much."

The little man accompanied these latter words with a wink, expressive of the estimate he had formed of the travelers' pocketbook.

To this Mr. Codlin, who had a surly, grumbling manner, replied, as he twitched Punch off the tombstone and flung him into the box:

"I don't care if we haven't lost a farden, but you're too free. If you stood in front of the curtain and see the public's faces as I do, you'd know human natur' better."

Turning over the figures in the box like one who knew and despised them, Mr. Codlin drew one forth and held it up for the inspection of his friend:

"Look here; here's all this Judy's clothes falling to pieces again. You haven't got a needle and thread, I suppose?"

The little man shook his head and scratched it sadly, as he contemplated this condition of a principal performer in his show. Seeing that they were at a loss, the child said, timidly:

"I have a needle, sir, in my basket, and thread too. Will you let me try to mend it for you? I think I could do it neater than you could."

Even Mr. Codlin had nothing to urge against a proposal so seasonable. Nell, kneeling down beside the box, was soon busily engaged in her task, and finished it in a wonderful way.

While she was thus at work, the merry little man looked at her with an interest which did not appear to be any less when he glanced at her helpless companion. When she had finished her work he thanked her, and asked to what place they were traveling.

"N—no farther to-night, I think," said the child, looking toward her grandfather.

"If you're wanting a place to stop at," the man remarked. "I should advise you to take up at the same house with us. That's it. The long low, white house there. It's very cheap."

They went to the little inn, and when they had been refreshed, the whole house hurried away into an empty stable where the show stood, and where, by the light of a few flaring candles stuck round a hoop which hung by a line from the ceiling, it was to be forthwith shown.

And now Mr. Thomas Codlin, after blowing away at the Pan's pipes, took his station on one side of the curtain which concealed the mover of the figures, and, putting his hands in his pockets, prepared to reply to all questions and remarks of Punch, and to make a pretence of being his most intimate private friend, of believing in him to the fullest and most unlimited extent, of knowing that Mr. Punch enjoyed day and night a merry and glorious life in that temple, and that he was at all times and under every circumstance the same wise and joyful person that all present then beheld him.

The whole performance was applauded until the old stable rang, and gifts were showered in with a liberality which testified yet more strongly to the general delight. Among the laughter none was more loud and frequent than the old man's. Nell's was unheard, for she, poor child, with her head drooping on his shoulder, had fallen asleep, and slept too soundly to be roused by any of his efforts to awaken her to a part in his glee.

The supper was very good, but she was too tired to eat, and yet would not leave the old man until she had kissed him in his bed. He, happily insensible to every care and anxiety, sat listening with a vacant smile and admiring face to all that his new friends said; and it was not until they retired yawning to their room that he followed the child up-stairs.

She had a little money, but it was very little; and when that was gone they must begin to beg. There was one piece of gold among it, and a need might come when its worth to them would be increased a hundred times. It would be best to hide this coin, and never show it unless their case was entirely desperate, and nothing else was left them.

Her resolution taken, she sewed the piece of gold into her dress, and going to bed with a lighter heart sunk into a deep slumber.

"And where are you going to-day?" said the little man the following morning, addressing himself to Nell.

"Indeed I hardly know—we have not made up our minds yet," replied the child.

"We're going on to the races," said the little man. "If that's your way and you like to have us for company, let us travel together. If you prefer going alone, only say the word and you'll find that we sha'n't trouble you."

"We'll go with you," said the old man. "Nell—with them, with them."

The child thought for a moment, and knowing that she must shortly beg, and could scarcely hope to do so at a better place than where crowds of rich ladies and gentlemen were met together for enjoyment, determined to go with these men so far. She therefore thanked the little man for his offer, and said, glancing timidly toward his friend, that they would if there was no objection to their staying with them as far as the race-town.

And with these men they traveled forward on the following day.

They made two long days' journey with their new companions, passing through villages and towns, and meeting upon one occasion with two young people walking upon stilts, who were also going to the races.

And now they had come to the time when they must beg their bread. Soon after sunrise the second morning, she stole out, and, rambling into some fields at a short distance, plucked a few wild roses and such humble flowers, purposing to make them into little nosegays and offer them to the ladies in the carriages when the company arrived. Her thoughts were not idle while she was thus busy; when she returned and was seated beside the old man, tying her flowers together, while the two men lay dozing in the corner, she plucked him by the sleeve, and, slightly glancing toward them, said in a low voice:

"Grandfather, don't look at those I talk of, and don't seem as if I spoke of anything but what I am about. What was that you told me before we left the old house? That if they knew what we were going to do, they would say that you were mad, and part us?"

The old man turned to her with a look of wild terror; but she checked him by a look, and bidding him hold some flowers while she tied them up, and so bringing her lips closer to his ear, said:

"I know that was what you told me. You needn't speak, dear. I recollect it very well. It was not likely that I should forget it. Grandfather, I have heard these men say they think that we have secretly left our friends, and mean to carry us before some gentleman and have us taken care of and sent back. If you let your hand tremble so, we can never get away from them, but if you're only quiet now, we shall do so easily."

"How?" muttered the old man. "Dear Nell, how? They will shut me up in a stone-room, dark and cold, and chain me up to the wall, Nell—flog me with whips, and never let me see thee more!"

"You're trembling again," said the child. "Keep close to me all day. Never mind them, don't look at them, but me. I shall find a time when we can steal away. When I do, mind you come with me, and do not stop or speak a word. Hush! That's all."

"Halloo! what are you up to, my dear?" said Mr. Codlin, raising his head, and yawning.

"Making some nosegays," the child replied; "I am going to try to sell some, these three days of the races. Will you have one—as a present, I mean?"

Mr. Codlin would have risen to receive it, but the child hurried toward him and placed it in his hand, and he stuck it in his buttonhole.

As the morning wore on, the tents at the race-course assumed a gayer and more brilliant appearance, and long lines of carriages came rolling softly on the turf. Black-eyed gipsy girls, their heads covered with showy handkerchiefs, came out to tell fortunes, and pale, slender women with wasted faces followed the footsteps of conjurers, and counted the sixpences with anxious eyes long before they were gained. As many of the children as could be kept within bounds were stowed away, with all the other signs of dirt and poverty, among the donkeys, carts, and horses; and as many as could not be thus disposed of ran in and out in all directions, crept between people's legs and carriage wheels, and came forth unharmed from under horses' hoofs. The dancing-dogs, the stilts, the little lady and the tall man, and all the other attractions, with organs out of number and bands innumerable, came out from the holes and corners in which they had passed the night, and flourished boldly in the sun.

Along the uncleared course, Short led his party, sounding the brazen trumpet and speaking in the voice of Punch; and at his heels went Thomas Codlin, bearing the show as usual, and keeping his eye on Nell and her grandfather, as they rather lingered in the rear. The child bore upon her arm the little basket with her flowers, and sometimes stopped, with timid and modest looks, to offer them at some gay carriage; but alas! there were many bolder beggars there, gipsies who promised husbands, and others skillful in their trade; and although some ladies smiled gently as they shook their heads, and others cried to the gentlemen beside them, "See what a pretty face!" they let the pretty face pass on, and never thought that it looked tired or hungry.

There was but one lady who seemed to understand the child, and she was one who sat alone in a handsome carriage, while two young men in dashing clothes, who had just stepped out from it, talked and laughed loudly at a little distance, appearing to forget her, quite. There were many ladies all around, but they turned their backs, or looked another way, or at the two young men (not unfavorably at *them*), and left her to herself. The lady motioned away a gipsy woman, eager to tell her fortune, saying that it was told already and had been for some years, but called the child toward her, and, taking her flowers, put money into her trembling hand, and bade her go home and keep at home.

Many a time they went up and down those long, long lines, seeing everything but the horses and the race; when the bell rung to clear the course, going back to rest among the carts and donkeys, and not coming out again until the heat was over. Many a time, too, was Punch displayed in the full glory of his humor; but all this while the eye of Thomas Codlin was upon them, and to escape without notice was almost impossible.

At length, late in the day, Mr. Codlin pitched the show in a spot right in the middle of the crowd, and the Punch and Judy were surrounded by people who were watching the performance.

Short was moving the images, and knocking them in the fury of the combat against the sides of the show, the people were looking on with laughing faces, and Mr. Codlin's face showed a grim smile as his roving eye detected the hands of thieves in the crowd going into waistcoat pockets. If Nell and her grandfather were ever to get away unseen, that was the very moment. They seized it, and fled.

They made a path through booths and carriages and throngs of people, and never once stopped to look behind. The bell was ringing, and the course was cleared by the time they reached the ropes, but they dashed across it, paying no attention to the shouts and screeching that assailed them for breaking in it, and, creeping under the brow of the hill at a quick pace, made for the open fields. At last they were free from Codlin and Short.

That night they reached a little village in a woody hollow. The village schoolmaster, a good and gentle man, pitying their weariness, and attracted by the child's sweetness and modesty, gave them a lodging for the night; nor would he let them leave him until two days more had passed.

They journeyed on, when the time came that they must wander forth again, by pleasant country lanes; and as they passed, watching the birds that perched and twittered in the branches overhead, or listening to the songs that broke the happy silence, their hearts were peaceful and free from care. But by-and-by they came to a long winding road which lengthened out far into the distance, and though they still kept on, it was at a much slower pace, for they were now very weary.

The afternoon had worn away into a beautiful evening, when they arrived at a point where the road made a sharp turn and struck across a common. On the border of this common, and close to the hedge which divided it from the cultivated fields, a caravan was drawn up to rest; upon which they came so suddenly that they could not have avoided it if they would. Do you know what a "caravan" is? It is a sort of gipsy house on wheels in which people live, while the house moves from place to place.

It was not a shabby, dingy, dusty cart, but a smart little house with white dimity curtains hung over the windows, and window-shutters of green picked out with panels of a staring red, in which happily-contrasted colors the whole house shone brilliant. Neither was it a poor caravan drawn by a single donkey or feeble old horse, for a pair of horses in pretty good condition were released from the shafts and grazing on the frouzy grass. Neither was it a gipsy caravan, for at the open door (graced with a bright brass knocker) sat a Christian lady, stout and comfortable to look upon, who wore a large bonnet trembling with bows. And that it was not a caravan of poor people was clear from what this lady was doing; for she was taking her tea. The tea-things, including a bottle of rather suspicious looks and a cold knuckle of ham, were set forth upon a drum, covered with a white napkin; and there, as if at the most convenient round-table in all the world, sat this roving lady, taking her tea and enjoying the prospect.

It happened at that moment that the lady of the caravan had her cup (which, that everything about her might be of a stout and comfortable kind, was a breakfast cup) to her lips, and that having her eyes lifted to the sky in her enjoyment of the full flavor of her tea, it happened that, being thus agreeably engaged, she did not see the travelers when they first came up. It was not until she was in the act of setting down the cup, and drawing a long breath after the exertion of swallowing its contents, that the lady of the caravan beheld an old man and a young child walking slowly by, and glancing at her proceedings with eyes of modest, but hungry admiration.

"Hey!" cried the lady of the caravan, scooping the crumbs out of her lap and swallowing the same before wiping her lips. "Yes, to be sure————Who won the Helter-Skelter Plate, child?"

"Won what, ma'am?" asked Nell.

"The Helter-Skelter Plate at the races, child—the plate that was run for on the second day."

"On the second day, ma'am?"

"Second day! Yes, second day," repeated the lady, with an air of impatience. "Can't you say who won the Helter-Skelter Plate when you're asked the question civilly?"

"I don't know, ma'am."

"Don't know!" repeated the lady of the caravan; "why, you were there. I saw you with my own eyes."

Nell was not a little alarmed to hear this, supposing that the lady might be intimately acquainted with the firm of Short and Codlin; but what followed tended to put her at her ease.

"And very sorry I was," said the lady of the caravan, "to see you in company with a Punch—a low, common, vulgar wretch, that people should scorn to look at."

"I was not there by choice," returned the child; "we didn't know our way, and the two men were very kind to us, and let us travel with them. Do you—do you know them, ma'am?"

"Know 'em, child?" cried the lady of the caravan, in a sort of shriek. "Know *them*! But you're young and ignorant, and that's your excuse for asking sich a question. Do I look as if I know'd 'em? does the caravan look as if *it* know'd 'em?"

"No, ma'am, no," said the child, fearing she had committed some grievous fault. "I beg your pardon."

The lady of the caravan was in the act of gathering her tea things together preparing to clear the table, but noting the child's anxious manner, she hesitated and stopped. The child courtesied, and, giving her hand to the old man, had already got some fifty yards or so away, when the lady of the caravan called to her to return.

"Come nearer, nearer still," said she, beckoning to her to ascend the steps. "Are you hungry, child?"

"Not very, but we are tired, and it's—it *is* a long way———"

"Well, hungry or not, you had better have some tea," rejoined her new acquaintance. "I suppose you are agreeable to that old gentleman?"

The grandfather humbly pulled off his hat and thanked her. The lady of the caravan then bade him come up the steps likewise, but the drum proving an inconvenient table for two, they went down again, and sat upon the grass, where she handed down to them the tea-tray, the bread and butter, and the knuckle of ham.

"Set 'em out near the hind wheels child, that's the best place," said their friend, superintending the arrangement from above. "Now hand up the tea-pot for a little more hot water and a pinch of fresh tea, and then both of you eat and drink as much as you can, and don't spare anything; that's all I ask of you."

The mistress of the caravan, saying the girl and her grandfather could not be very heavy, invited them to go along with them for a while, for which Nell thanked her with all her heart.

When they had traveled slowly forward for some short distance, Nell ventured to steal a look round the caravan and observe it more closely. One-half of it—that part in which the comfortable proprietress was then seated—was carpeted, and so divided the farther end as to form a sleeping-place, made after the fashion of a berth on board ship, which was shaded, like the little windows, with fair white curtains, and looked comfortable enough, though by what kind of gymnastic exercise the lady of the caravan ever contrived to get into it was a mystery. The other half served for a kitchen, and was fitted up with a stove whose small chimney passed through the roof.

The mistress sat looking at the child for a long time in silence, and then, getting up, brought out from a corner a large roll of canvas about a yard in width, which she laid upon the floor and spread open with her foot until it nearly reached from one end of the caravan to the other.

"There, child," she said, "read that."

Nell walked down it, and read aloud, in enormous black letters, the inscription, "JARLEY'S WAX-WORK."

"Read it again," said the lady, complacently.

"Jarley's Wax-work," repeated Nell.

"That's me," said the lady. "I am Mrs. Jarley."

Giving the child an encouraging look, the lady of the caravan unfolded another scroll, whereon was the inscription, "One hundred figures the full size of life;" and then another scroll, on which was written, "The only stupendous collection of real wax-work in the world;" and then several smaller scrolls, with such inscriptions as "Now exhibiting within"—"The genuine and only Jarley"—"Jarley's unrivaled collection"—"Jarley is the delight of the Nobility and Gentry"—"The Royal Family are the patrons of Jarley." When she had exhibited these large painted signs to the astonished child, she brought forth specimens of the lesser notices in the shape of hand-bills, some of which were printed in the form of verses on popular times, as "Believe me if all Jarley's wax-work so rare"—"I saw thy show in youthful prime"—"Over the water to Jarley;" while, to satisfy all tastes, others were composed with a view to the lighter and merrier spirits, as a verse on the favorite air of "If I had a donkey," beginning

> If I know'd a donkey wot wouldn't go
> To see Mrs. Jarley's wax-work show,
> Do you think I'd own him?
> Oh no, no!
>
> Then run to Jarley's——

besides several compositions in prose, pretending to be dialogues between the Emperor of China and an oyster.

"I never saw any wax-work, ma'am," said Nell. "Is it funnier than Punch?"

"Funnier!" said Mrs. Jarley in a shrill voice. "It is not funny at all."

"Oh!" said Nell, with all possible humility.

"It isn't funny at all," repeated Mrs. Jarley. "It's calm and—what's that word again—critical?—no—classical, that's it—it's calm and classical. No low beatings and knockings about, no jokings and squeakings like your precious Punches, but always the same, with a constantly unchanging air of coldness and dignity; and so like life that, if wax-work only spoke and walked about you'd hardly know the difference. I won't go so far as to say that, as it is, I've seen wax-work quite like life, but I've certainly seen some life that was exactly like wax-work."

This conference at length concluded, she beckoned Nell to sit down.

"And the old gentleman, too," said Mrs. Jarley; "for I want to have a word with him. Do you want a good place for your granddaughter, master? If you do, I can put her in the way of getting one. What do you say?"

"I can't leave her," answered the old man. "We can't separate. What would become of me without her?"

"If you're really ready to employ yourself," said Mrs. Jarley, "there would be plenty for you to do in the way of helping to dust the figures, and take the checks, and so forth. What I want your granddaughter for is to point 'em out to the company; they would be soon learned and she has a way with her that people wouldn't think unpleasant, though she *does* come after me; for I've been always accustomed to go round with visitors myself, which I should keep on doing now, only that my spirits make a little rest absolutely necessary. It's not a common offer, bear in mind," said the lady, rising into the tone and manner in which she was accustomed to address her audiences; "it's Jarley's wax-work, remember. The duty's very light and genteel, the company particularly select, the exhibition takes place in assembly-rooms, town-halls, large rooms at inns, or auction galleries. There is none of your open-air wondering at Jarley's, recollect; there is no tarpaulin and sawdust at Jarley's, remember. Every promise made in the hand-bills is kept to the utmost, and the whole forms an effect of splendor hitherto unknown in this kingdom. Remember that the price of admission is only sixpence, and that this is an opportunity which may never occur again!"

"We are very much obliged to you, ma'am," said Nell, "and thankfully accept your offer."

"And you'll never be sorry for it," returned Mrs. Jarley. "I'm pretty sure of that. So as that's all settled, let us have a bit of supper."

Rumbling along with most unwonted noise, the caravan stopped at last at the place of exhibition, where Nell came down from the wagon among an admiring group of children, who evidently supposed her to be an important part of the curiosities, and were almost ready to believe that her grandfather was a cunning device in wax. The chests were taken out of the van for the figures with all haste, and taken in to be unlocked by Mrs. Jarley, who, attended by George and the driver, arranged their contents (consisting of red festoons and other ornamental work) to make the best show in the decoration of the room.

When the festoons were all put up as tastily as they might be, the wonderful collection was uncovered; and there were shown, on a raised platform some two feet from the floor, running round the room and parted from the rude public by a crimson rope, breast high, a large number of sprightly waxen images of famous people, singly and in groups, clad in glittering dresses of various climes and times, and standing more or less unsteadily upon their legs, with their eyes very wide open, and their nostrils very much inflated, and the muscles of their legs, and arms very strongly developed, and all their faces expressing great surprise. All the gentlemen were very narrow in the breast, and very blue about the beards; and all the ladies were wonderful figures; and all the ladies and all the gentlemen were looking intensely nowhere, and staring with tremendous earnestness at nothing.

When Nell had shown her first wonder at this glorious sight, Mrs. Jarley ordered the room to be cleared of all but herself and the child, and, sitting herself down in an arm-chair in the center, presented Nell with a willow wand, long used by herself for pointing out the characters, and was at great pains to instruct her in her duty.

"That," said Mrs. Jarley, in her exhibition tone, as Nell touched a figure at the beginning of the platform, "is an unfortunate maid of honor in the time of Queen Elizabeth, who died from pricking her finger in consequence of working upon a Sunday. Observe the blood which is trickling from her finger; also the gold-eyed needle of the period, with which she is at work."

All this Nell repeated twice or thrice—pointing to the finger and the needle at the right times; and then passed on to the next.

"That, ladies and gentlemen," said Mrs. Jarley, "is Jasper Packlemerton, of terrible memory, who courted and married fourteen wives, and destroyed them all, by tickling the soles of their feet when they were sleeping in the consciousness of innocence and virtue. On being brought to the scaffold and asked if he was sorry for what he had done, he replied yes, he was sorry for having let 'em off so easy, and hoped all Christian husbands would pardon him the offense. Let this be a warning to all young ladies to be particular in the character of the gentlemen of their choice. Observe that his fingers are curled as if in the act of tickling, and that his face is represented with a wink, as he appeared when committing his barbarous murders."

When Nell knew all about Mr. Packlemerton, and could say it without faltering, Mrs. Jarley passed on to the fat man, and then to the thin man, the tall man, the short man, the old lady who died of dancing at a hundred and thirty-two, the wild boy of the woods, the woman who poisoned fourteen families with pickled walnuts, and other historical characters and interesting but misguided individuals. And so well did Nell profit by her instructions, and so apt was she to remember them, that by the time they had been shut up together for a couple of hours, she was in full possession of the history of the whole establishment, and perfectly able to tell the stories of the wax-work to visitors.

For some time her life and the life of the poor vacant old man passed quietly and happily. They traveled from place to place with Mrs. Jarley; Nell spoke her piece, with the wand in her hand, before the waxen images; and her grandfather in a dull way dusted the images when he was told to do so.

But heavier sorrow was yet to come. One night, a holiday night for them, Neil and her grandfather went out to walk. A terrible thunderstorm coming on, they were forced to take refuge in a small public house; and here they saw some shabbily dressed and wicked looking men were playing cards. The old man watched them with increasing interest and excitement, until his whole appearance underwent a complete change. His face was flushed and eager, his teeth set. With a hand that trembled violently he seized Nell's little purse, and in spite of her pleadings joined in the game, gambling with such a savage thirst for gain that the distressed and frightened child could almost better have borne to see him dead. It was long after midnight when the play came to an end; and they were forced to remain where they were until the morning. And in the night the child was wakened from her troubled sleep to find a figure in the room—a figure busying its hands about her garments, while its face was turned to her, listening and looking lest she should awake. It was her grandfather himself, his white face pinched and sharpened by the greediness which made his eyes unnaturally bright, counting the money of which his hands were robbing her.

Evening after evening, after that night, the old man would steal away, not to return until the night was far spent, demanding, wildly, money. And at last there came an hour when the child overheard him, tempted beyond his feeble powers of resistance, undertake to find more money to feed the desperate passion which had laid its hold upon his weakness by robbing the kind Mrs. Jarley, who had done so much for them. The poor old man had become so weak in his mind, that he did not understand how wicked was his act.

That night the child took her grandfather by the hand and led him forth. Through the strait streets and narrow outskirts of the town their trembling feet passed quickly; the child sustained by one idea—that they were flying from wickedness and disgrace, and that she could save her grandfather only by her firmness unaided by one word of advice or any helping hand; the old man following her as though she had been an angel messenger sent to lead him where she would.

The hardest part of all their wanderings was now before them. They slept in the open air that night, and on the following morning some men offered to take them a long distance on their barge on the river. These men, though they were not unkindly, were very rugged, noisy fellows, and they drank and quarreled fearfully among themselves, to Nell's inexpressible terror. It rained, too, heavily, and she was wet and cold. At last they reached the great city whither the barge was bound, and here they wandered up and down, being now penniless, and watched the faces of those who passed, to find among them a ray of encouragement or hope. Ill in body, and sick to death at heart, the child needed her utmost courage and will even to creep along.

They lay down that night, and the next night too, with nothing between them and the sky; a penny loaf was all they had had that day, and when the third morning came, it found the child much weaker, yet she made no complaint. The great city with its many factories hemmed them in on every side, and seemed to shut out hope.

Faint and spiritless as they were, its streets were terrible to them. After humbly asking for relief at some few doors, and being driven away, they agreed to make their way out of it as speedily as they could, and try if the people living in some lone house beyond would have more pity on their worn out state.

They were dragging themselves along through the last street, and the child felt that the time was close at hand when her enfeebled powers would bear no more. There appeared before them, at this moment, going in the same direction as themselves, a traveler on foot, who, with a bundle of clothing strapped to his back, leaned upon a stout stick as he walked, and read from a book which he held in his other hand.

It was not an easy matter to come up with him and ask his aid, for he walked fast, and was a little distance in advance. At length he stopped, to look more attentively at some passage in his book. Encouraged by a ray of hope, the child shot on before her grandfather, and, going close to the stranger without rousing him by the sound of her footsteps, began, in a few faint words, to beg his help.

He turned his head. The child clapped her hands together, uttered a wild shriek, and fell senseless at his feet.

It was the poor schoolmaster. No other than the poor schoolmaster. Scarcely less moved and surprised by the sight of the child than she had been on recognizing him, he stood, for a moment, silent, without even the presence of mind to raise her from the ground.

But, quickly recovering himself, he threw down his stick and book, and, dropping on one knee beside her, tried simple means as came to his mind, to restore her to herself; while her grandfather, standing idly by, wrung his hands, and begged her, with many words of love, to speak to him, were it only a whisper.

"She appears to be quite worn out," said the schoolmaster, glancing upward into his face. "You have used up all her strength, friend."

"She is dying of want," answered the old man. "I never thought how weak and ill she was till now."

Casting a look upon him, half-angry and half-pitiful, the schoolmaster took the child in his arms, and, bidding the old man gather up her little basket and follow him directly, bore her away at his utmost speed.

There was a small inn within sight, to which, it would seem, he had been walking when so unexpectedly overtaken. Toward this place he hurried with his unconscious burden, and rushing into the kitchen, and calling upon the company there assembled to make way for God's sake, laid it down on a chair before the fire.

The company, who rose in confusion on the schoolmaster's entrance, did as people usually do under such circumstances. Everybody called for his or her favorite remedy, which nobody brought; each cried for more air, at the same time carefully shutting out what air there was, by closing round the object of sympathy; and all wondered why somebody else didn't do what it never appeared to occur to them might be done by themselves.

The landlady, however, who had more readiness and activity than any of them, and who seemed to understand the case more quickly, soon came running in, with a little hot medicine, followed by her servant-girl, carrying vinegar, hartshorn, smelling-salts, and such other restoratives; which, being duly given, helped the child so far as to enable her to thank them in a faint voice, and to hold out her hand to the poor schoolmaster, who stood, with an anxious face, near her side. Without suffering her to speak another word, or so much as to stir a finger any more, the women straightway carried her off to bed; and, having covered her up warm, bathed her cold feet, and wrapped them in flannel, they sent a messenger for the doctor.

The doctor, who was a red-nosed gentleman with a great bunch of seals dangling below a waistcoat of ribbed black satin, arrived with all speed, and taking his seat by the bedside of poor Nell, drew out his watch, and felt her pulse. Then he looked at her tongue, then he felt her pulse again, and while he did so, he eyed the half-emptied wine-glass as if in profound abstraction.

"I should give her," said the doctor at length, "a teaspoonful, every now and then, of hot medicine."

"Why, that's exactly what we've done, sir!" said the delighted landlady.

"I should also," observed the doctor, who had passed the foot-bath on the stairs, "I should also," said the doctor, in a very wise tone of voice, "put her feet in hot water and wrap them up in flannel. I should likewise," said the doctor, with increased solemnity, "give her something light for supper—the wing of a roasted chicken now———"

"Why, goodness gracious me, sir, it's cooking at the kitchen fire this instant!" cried the landlady. And so indeed it was, for the schoolmaster had ordered it to be put down, and it was getting on so well that the doctor might have smelled it if he had tried; perhaps he did.

"You may then," said the doctor, rising gravely, "give her a glass of hot mulled port-wine, if she likes wine———"

"And a piece of toast, sir?" suggested the landlady.

"Ay," said the doctor, in a very dignified tone, "And a toast— of bread. But be very particular to make it of bread, if you please, ma'am."

With which parting advice, slowly and solemnly given, the doctor departed, leaving the whole house in admiration of that wisdom which agreed so closely with their own. Everybody said he was a very shrewd doctor indeed, and knew perfectly what people's bodies needed; which there appears some reason to suppose he did.

While her supper was preparing, the child fell into a refreshing sleep, from which they were obliged to rouse her when it was ready. As she showed extraordinary uneasiness on learning that her grandfather was below stairs, and as she was greatly troubled at the thought of their being apart, he took his supper with her. Finding her still very anxious for the old man, they made him up a bed in an inner room, to which he soon went. The key of this room happened by good-fortune to be on that side of the door which was in Nell's room; she turned it on him when the landlady had withdrawn, and crept to bed again with a thankful heart.

The schoolmaster sat for a long time smoking his pipe by the kitchen fire, which was now deserted, thinking, with a very happy face, on the fortunate chance which had brought him at just the right moment to the child's assistance.

The schoolmaster, as it appeared, was on his way to a new home. And when the child had recovered somewhat from her hunger and weariness, it was arranged that she and her grandfather should go with him to the village whither he was bound, and that he should endeavor to find them some work by which they could get their living.

It was a lonely little village, lying among the quiet country scenes Nell loved. And here, her grandfather being peaceful and at rest, a great calm fell upon the spirit of the child. Often she would steal into the church, and, sitting down among the quiet figures carved upon the tombs, would think of the summer days and the bright springtime that would come; of the rays of sun that would fall in, aslant those sleeping forms; of the songs of birds, and the sweet air that would steal in. What if the spot awakened thoughts of death! It would be no pain to sleep amid such sights and sounds as these. For the time was drawing nearer every day when Nell was to rest indeed. She never murmured or complained, but faded like a light upon a summer's evening and died. Day after day and all day long, the old man, broken-hearted and with no love or care for anything in life, would sit beside her grave with her straw hat and the little basket she had been used to carry, waiting till she should come to him again. At last they found him lying dead upon the stone. And in the church where they had often prayed and mused and lingered, hand in hand, the child and the old man slept together.

VII

Little David Copperfield

I, little David Copperfield, lived with my mother in a pretty house in the village of Blunderstone in Suffolk. I had never known my father, who died before I could remember anything, and I had neither brothers nor sisters. I was fondly loved by my pretty young mother, and our kind, good servant, Peggotty, and was a very happy little fellow. We had very few friends, and the only relation my mother talked about was an aunt of my father's, a tall and rather terrible old lady, from all accounts, who had once been to see us when I was quite a tiny baby, and had been so angry to find I was not a little girl that she had left the house quite offended, and had never been heard of since. One visitor, a tall dark gentleman, I did not like at all, and was rather inclined to be jealous that my mother should be so friendly with the stranger.

Peggotty and I were sitting one night by the parlor fire, alone. I had been reading to Peggotty about crocodiles. I was tired of reading, and dead sleepy; but having leave, as a high treat, to sit up until my mother came home from spending the evening at a neighbor's, I would rather have died upon my post (of course) than have gone to bed. I had reached that stage of sleepiness when Peggotty seemed to swell and grow immensely large. I propped my eyelids open with my two forefingers, and looked perseveringly at her as she sat at work; at the little house with a thatched roof, where she kept her yard-measure; at her work-box with a sliding-lid, with a view of St. Paul's Cathedral (with a pink dome) painted on the top; at the brass thimble on her finger; at herself, whom I thought lovely. I felt so sleepy that I knew if I lost sight of anything, for a moment, I was gone.

"Peggotty," says I, suddenly, "were you ever married?"

"Lord, Master Davy!" replied Peggotty. "What's put marriage in your head?"

She answered with such a start that it quite awoke me. And then she stopped in her work and looked at me, with her needle drawn out to its thread's length.

"But *were* you ever married, Peggotty?" says I. "You are a very handsome woman, ain't you?"

"Me handsome, Davy!" said Peggotty. "Lawk, no, my dear! But what put marriage in your head?"

"I don't know! You mustn't marry more than one person at a time, may you, Peggotty?"

"Certainly not," says Peggotty, with the promptest decision.

"But if you marry a person, and the person dies, why then you may marry another person, mayn't you, Peggotty?"

"You MAY," says Peggotty, "if you choose, my dear. That's a matter of opinion."

"But what is your opinion, Peggotty?" said I.

I asked her and looked curiously at her, because she looked so curiously at me.

"My opinion is," said Peggotty, taking her eyes from me, after waiting a little, and going on with her work, "that I never was married myself, Master Davy, and that I don't expect to be. That's all I know about the subject."

"You ain't cross, I suppose, Peggotty, are you?" said I, after sitting quiet for a minute.

I really thought she was, she had been so short with me; but I was quite mistaken; for she laid aside her work (which was a stocking of her own) and opening her arms wide, took my curly head within them, and gave it a good squeeze. I know it was a good squeeze, because, being very plump, whenever she made any little exertion after she was dressed, some of the buttons on the back of her flew off. And I recollect two bursting to the opposite side of the parlor while she was hugging me.

One day Peggotty asked me if I would like to go with her on a visit to her brother at Yarmouth.

"Is your brother an agreeable man, Peggotty?" I inquired.

"Oh, what an agreeable man he is!" cried Peggotty. "Then there's the sea, and the boats and ships, and the fishermen, and the beach. And 'Am to play with."

Ham was her nephew. I was quite anxious to go when I heard of all these delights; but my mother, what would she do all alone? Peggotty told me my mother was going to pay a visit to some friends, and would be sure to let me go. So all was arranged, and we were to start the next day in the carrier's cart. I was so eager that I wanted to put my hat and coat on the night before! But when the time came to say good-by to my dear mamma, I cried a little, for I had never left her before. It was rather a slow way of traveling, and I was very tired and sleepy when I arrived at Yarmouth, and found Ham waiting to meet me. He was a great strong fellow, six feet high, and took me on his back and the box under his arm to carry both to the house. I was delighted to find that this house was made of a real big black boat, with a door and windows cut in the side, and an iron funnel sticking out of the roof for a chimney. Inside, it was very cozy and clean, and I had a tiny bedroom in the stern. I was very much pleased to find a dear little girl, about my own age, to play with, and after tea I said:

"Mr. Peggotty."

"Sir," says he.

"Did you give your son the name of Ham because you lived in a sort of ark?"

Mr. Peggotty seemed to think it a deep idea, but answered:

"No, sir. I never giv' him no name."

"Who gave him that name, then?" said I, putting question number two of the catechism to Mr. Peggotty.

"Why, sir, his father giv' it him," said Mr. Peggotty.

"I thought you were his father!"

"My brother Joe was *his* father," said Mr. Peggotty.

"Dead, Mr. Peggotty?" I hinted, after a respectful pause.

"Drowndead," said Mr. Peggotty.

I was very much surprised that Mr. Peggotty was not Ham's father, and began to wonder whether I was mistaken about his relationship to anybody else there. I was so curious to know that I made up my mind to have it out with Mr. Peggotty.

"Little Em'ly," I said, glancing at her. "She is your daughter, isn't she, Mr. Peggotty?"

"No, sir. My brother-in-law, Tom, was *her* father."

I couldn't help it. "——Dead, Mr. Peggotty?" I hinted, after another respectful silence.

"Drowndead," said Mr. Peggotty.

I felt the difficulty of resuming the subject, but had not got to the bottom of it yet, and must get to the bottom somehow. So I said:

"Haven't you *any* children, Mr. Peggotty?"

"No, master," he answered, with a short laugh. "I'm a bacheldore."

"A bachelor!" I said, astonished. "Why, who's that, Mr. Peggotty?" Pointing to the person in the apron who was knitting.

"That's Missis Gummidge," said Mr. Peggotty.

"Gummidge, Mr. Peggotty?"

But at this point Peggotty—I mean my own Peggotty—made such impressive motions to me not to ask any more questions, that I could only sit and look at all the company, until it was time to go to bed.

Mrs. Gummidge lived with them too, and did the cooking and cleaning, for she was a poor widow and had no home of her own. I thought Mr. Peggotty was very good to take all these people to live with him, and I was quite right, for Mr. Peggotty was only a poor man himself and had to work hard to get a living.

Almost as soon as morning shone upon the oyster-shell frame of my mirror I was out of bed, and out with tittle Em'ly, picking up stones upon the beach.

"You're quite a sailor I suppose?" I said to Em'ly. I don't know that I supposed anything of the kind, but I felt it proper to say something; and a shining sail close to us made such a pretty little image of itself, at the moment, in her bright eye, that it came into my head to say this.

"No," replied Em'ly, shaking her head, "I'm afraid of the sea."

"Afraid!" I said, with a becoming air of boldness, and looking very big at the mighty ocean. "I ain't."

"Ah! but it's cruel," said Em'ly. "I have seen it very cruel to some of our men. I have seen it tear a boat as big as our house all to pieces."

"I hope it wasn't the boat that—"

"That father was drowned in?" said Em'ly. "No. Not that one, I never see that boat."

"Nor him?" I asked her.

Little Em'ly shook her head. "Not to remember!"

Here was something remarkable. I immediately went into an explanation how I had never seen my own father; and how my mother and I had always lived by ourselves in the happiest state imaginable, and lived so then, and always meant to live so; and how my father's grave was in the churchyard near our house, and shaded by a tree, beneath the boughs of which I had walked and heard the birds sing many a pleasant morning. But there were some differences between Em'ly's orphanhood and mine, it appeared. She had lost her mother before her father, and where her father's grave was no one knew, except that it was somewhere in the depths of the sea.

"Besides," said Em'ly, as she looked about for shells and pebbles, "your father was a gentleman and your mother is a lady; and my father was a fisherman and my mother was a fisherman's daughter, and my Uncle Dan is a fisherman."

"Dan is Mr. Peggotty, is he?" said I.

David Copperfield and Little Em'ly

"Uncle—yonder," answered Em'ly, nodding at the boat-house.

"Yes. I mean him. He must be very good, I should think."

"Good?" said Em'ly. "If I was ever to be a lady, I'd give him a sky-blue coat with diamond buttons, nankeen trousers, a red velvet waistcoat, a cocked hat, a large gold watch, a silver pipe, and a box of money."

I said I had no doubt that Mr. Peggotty well deserved these treasures.

Little Em'ly had stopped and looked up at the sky while she named these articles, as if they were a glorious vision. We went on again picking up shells and pebbles.

"You would like to be a lady?" I said.

Em'ly looked at me, and laughed and nodded "yes."

"I should like it very much. We would all be gentlefolks together, then. Me, and uncle, and Ham, and Mrs. Gummidge. We wouldn't mind then, when there come stormy weather. Not for our own sakes, I mean. We would for the poor fishermen's, to be sure, and we'd help 'em with money when they come to any hurt."

I was quite sorry to leave these kind people and my dear little companion, but I was glad to think I should get back to my own dear mamma. When I reached home, however, I found a great change. My mother was married to the dark man I did not like, whose name was Mr. Murdstone, and he was a stern, hard man, who had no love for me, and did not allow my mother to pet and indulge me as she had done before. Mr. Murdstone's sister came to live with us, and as she was even more difficult to please than her brother, and disliked boys, my life was no longer a happy one. I tried to be good and obedient, for I knew it made my mother very unhappy to see me punished and found fault with. I had always had lessons with my mother, and as she was patient and gentle, I had enjoyed learning to read, but now I had a great many very hard lessons to do, and was so frightened and shy when Mr. and Miss Murdstone were in the room, that I did not get on at all well, and was continually in disgrace.

Let me remember how it used to be, and bring one morning back again.

I come into the second-best parlor after breakfast, with my books, and an exercise-book and a slate. My mother is ready for me at her writing-desk, but not half so ready as Mr. Murdstone in his easy-chair by the window (though he pretends to be reading a book), or as Miss Murdstone, sitting near my mother stringing steel beads. The very sight of these two has such an influence over me that I begin to feel the words I have been at infinite pains to get into my head all sliding away, and going I don't know where. I wonder where they *do* go, by-the-by?

I hand the first book to my mother. Perhaps it is a grammar, per-haps a history, or geography. I take a last drowning look at the page as I give it into her hand, and start off aloud at a racing pace while I have got it fresh. I trip over a word. Mr. Murdstone looks up. I trip over another word. Miss Murdstone looks up. I redden, tumble over half a dozen words and stop. I think my mother would show me the book if she dared, but she does not dare, and she says softly:

"Oh, Davy, Davy!"

"Now, Clara," says Mr. Murdstone, "be firm with the boy. Don't say, 'Oh, Davy, Davy!' That's childish. He knows his lesson, or he does not know it."

"He does *not* know it," Miss Murdstone interposes awfully.

"I am really afraid he does not," says my mother.

"Then you see, Clara," returns Miss Murdstone, "you should just give him the book back, and make him know it."

"Yes, certainly," says my mother; "that is what I intend to do, my dear Jane. Now, Davy, try once more, and don't be stupid."

I obey the first clause of my mother's words by trying once more, but am not so successful with the second, for I am very stupid. I tumble down before I get to the old place, at a point where I was all right before, and stop to think. But I can't think about the lesson. I think of the number of yards of net in Miss Murdstone's cap, or of the price of Mr. Murdstone's dressing-gown, or any such ridiculous matter that I have no business with, and don't want to have anything at all to do with. Mr. Murdstone makes a movement of impatience which I have been expecting for a long time. Miss Murdstone does the same. My mother glances submissively at them, shuts the book, and lays it by, to be worked out when my other tasks are done.

There is a pile of these tasks very soon, and it swells like a rolling snowball. The bigger it gets, the more stupid *I* get. The case is so hopeless, and I feel that I am wallowing in such a bog of nonsense, that I give up all idea of getting out, and abandon myself to my fate. The despairing way in which my mother and I look at each other, as I blunder on, is truly melancholy. But the greatest effect in these miserable lessons is when my mother (thinking nobody is observing her) tries to give me the cue by the motion of her lips. At that instant, Miss Murdstone, who has been lying in wait for nothing else all along says in a deep warning voice:

"Clara!"

My mother starts, colors, and smiles faintly. Mr. Murdstone comes out of his chair, takes the book, throws it at me, or boxes my ears with it, and turns me out of the room by the shoulders.

My only pleasure was to go up into a little room at the top of the house where I had found a number of books that had belonged to my own father, and I would sit and read Robinson Crusoe, and many tales of travels and adventures, and I imagined myself to be sometimes one and sometimes another hero, and went about for days with the centre-piece out of an old set of boot-trees, pretending to be a captain in the British Royal Navy.

One morning when I went into the parlor with my books, I found my mother looking anxious, Miss Murdstone looking firm, and Mr. Murdstone binding something round the bottom of a cane—a lithe and limber cane, which he left off binding when I came in, and poised and switched in the air.

"I tell you, Clara," said Mr. Murdstone, "I have often been flogged myself."

"To be sure; of course," said Miss Murdstone.

"Certainly, my dear Jane," faltered my mother, meekly. "But—but do you think it did Edward good?"

"Do you think it did Edward harm, Clara?" asked Mr. Murdstone, gravely.

"That's the point!" said his sister.

To this my mother returned, "Certainly, my dear Jane," and said no more.

I felt afraid that all this had something to do with myself, and sought Mr. Murdstone's eye as it lighted on mine.

"Now, David," he said—and I saw that cast again, as he said it—"you must be far more careful to-day than usual." He gave the cane another poise and another switch; and having finished his preparation of it, laid it down beside him, with an expressive look, and took up his book.

This was a good freshener to my memory, as a beginning. I felt the words of my lessons slipping off, not one by one, or line by line, but by the entire page. I tried to lay hold of them; but they seemed, if I may so express it, to have put skates on, and to skim away from me with a smoothness there was no checking.

We began badly, and went on worse. I had come in with an idea of doing better than usual, thinking that I was very well prepared; but it turned out to be quite a mistake. Book after book was added to the heap of failures, Miss Murdstone being firmly watchful of us all the time. And when we came at last to a question about five thousand cheeses (canes he made it that day, I remember), my mother burst out crying.

"Clara!" said Miss Murdstone, in her warning voice.

"I am not quite well, my dear Jane, I think," said my mother.

I saw him wink, solemnly, at his sister, as he rose and said, taking up the cane:

"Why, Jane, we can hardly expect Clara to bear, with perfect firmness, the worry and torment that David has caused her to-day. Clara is greatly strengthened and improved; but we can hardly expect so much from her. David, you and I will go up-stairs, boy."

As he took me out at the door, my mother ran towards us. Miss Murdstone said, "Clara! are you a perfect fool?" and interfered. I saw my mother stop her ears then, and I heard her crying.

He walked me up to my room slowly and gravely—I am certain he had a delight in that formal show of doing justice—and when we got there, suddenly twisted my head under his arm.

"Mr. Murdstone! Sir!" I cried to him. "Don't! Pray don't beat me! I have tried to learn, sir, but I can't learn while you and Miss Murdstone are by. I can't indeed!"

"Can't you, indeed, David?" he said. "We'll try that."

He had my head as in a vise, but I twined round him somehow, and stopped him for a moment, entreating him not to beat me. It was only for a moment that I stopped him, for he cut me heavily an instant afterwards, and in the same instant I caught the hand with which he held me in my mouth, between my teeth, and bit it through. It sets my teeth on edge to think of it.

He beat me then, as if he would have beaten me to death. Above all the noise we made, I heard them running up the stairs, and crying out—I heard my mother crying out—and Peggotty. Then he was gone; and the door was locked outside; and I was lying, fevered, and hot, and torn, and raging in my puny way, upon the floor.

How well I recollect, when I became quiet, what an unnatural stillness seemed to reign through the whole house! How well I remember, when my smart and passion began to cool, how wicked I began to feel!

I sat listening for a long while, but there was not a sound. I crawled up from the floor, and saw my face in the glass, so swollen, red, and ugly that it almost frightened me. My stripes were sore and stiff, and made me cry afresh, when I moved; but they were nothing to the guilt I felt. It lay heavier on my breast than if I had been a most terrible criminal, I dare say, and the longer I thought of it the greater the offense seemed.

It had begun to grow dark, and I had shut the window (I had been lying, for the most part, with my head upon the sill, by turns crying, dozing, and looking listlessly out), when the key was turned, and Miss Murdstone came in with some bread and meat and milk. These she put down upon the table without a word, glaring at me the while and then retired, locking the door after her.

I never shall forget the waking next morning; the being cheerful and fresh for the first moment, and then the being weighed down by the stale and dismal oppression of remembrance. Miss. Murdstone came again before I was out of bed; told me, in so many words, that I was free to walk in the garden for half an hour and no longer; retired, leaving the door open, that I might avail myself of that permission.

I did so, and did so every morning of my imprisonment, which lasted five days. If I could have seen my mother alone, I should have gone down on my knees to her and besought her forgiveness; but I saw no one, Miss Murdstone excepted, during the whole time.

The length of those five days I can convey no idea of to anyone. They occupy the place of years in my remembrance.

On the last night of my restraint, I was awakened by hearing my own name spoken in a whisper. I started up in bed, and, putting out my arms in the dark, said:

"Is that you, Peggotty?"

There was no immediate answer, but presently I heard my name again, in a tone so very mysterious and awful, that I think I should have gone into a fit, if it had not occurred to me that it must have come through the keyhole.

I groped my way to the door, and, putting my own lips to the keyhole, whispered:

"Is that you, Peggotty, dear?"

"Yes, my own precious Davy," she replied. "Be as soft as a mouse, or the cat'll hear us."

I understood this to mean Miss Murdstone, and knew that we must be careful and quiet; her room being close by.

"How's mamma, dear Peggotty? Is she very angry with me?"

I could hear Peggotty crying softly on her side of the keyhole, as I was doing on mine, before she answered. "No. Not very."

"What is going to be done with me, Peggotty, dear? Do you know?"

"School. Near London," was Peggotty's answer. I was obliged to get her to repeat it, for she spoke it the first time quite down my throat in consequence of my having forgotten to take my mouth away from the keyhole and put my ear there; and, though her words tickled me a good deal, I didn't hear them.

"When, Peggotty?"

"To-morrow."

"Is that the reason why Miss Murdstone took the clothes out of my drawers?" which she had done, though I have forgotten to mention it.

"Yes," said Peggotty. "Box."

"Shan't I see mamma?"

"Yes," said Peggotty. "Morning."

Then Peggotty fitted her mouth close to the keyhole, and spoke these words through it with as much feeling and earnestness as a keyhole has ever been the means of communicating, I will venture to say, shooting in each broken little sentence in a convulsive little burst of its own.

"Davy, dear. If I ain't been azackly as intimate with you. Lately, as I used to be. It ain't because I don't love you. Just as well and more, my pretty poppet. It's because I thought it better for you. And for someone else besides. Davy, my darling, are you listening? Can you hear?"

"Ye—ye—ye—yes, Peggotty!" I sobbed.

"My own!" said Peggotty, with infinite compassion. "What I want to say, is. That you must never forget me. For I'll never forget you. And I'll take as much care of your mamma, Davy. As I ever took of you. And I won't leave her. The day may come when she'll be glad to lay her poor head. On her stupid, cross old Peggotty's arm again. And I'll write to you, my dear. Though I ain't no scholar. And I'll—I'll—" Peggotty fell to kissing the keyhole, as she couldn't kiss me.

"Thank you, dear Peggotty!" said I. "Oh, thank you! Thank you! Will you promise me one thing, Peggotty? Will you write and tell Mr. Peggotty and little Em'ly and Mrs. Gummidge and Ham that I am not so bad as they might suppose, and that I sent 'em all my love—especially to little Em'ly? Will you, if you please, Peggotty?"

The kind soul promised, and we both of us kissed the keyhole with the greatest affection—I patted it with my hand, I recollect, as if it had been her honest face—and parted.

In the morning Miss Murdstone appeared as usual, and told me I was going to school; which was not altogether such news to me as she supposed. She also informed me that when I was dressed, I was to come down-stairs into the parlor and have my breakfast. There I found my mother, very pale and with red eyes; into whose arms I ran, and begged her pardon from my suffering soul.

"Oh, Davy!" she said. "That you could hurt anyone I love! Try to be better, pray to be better! I forgive you; but I am so grieved, Davy, that you should have such bad passions in your heart."

Miss Murdstone was good enough to take me out to the cart, and to say on the way that she hoped I would repent, before I came to a bad end; and then I got into the cart, and the lazy horse walked off with it.

We might have gone about half a mile, and my pocket handkerchief was quite wet through, when the carrier stopped short.

Looking out to ascertain for what, I saw, to my amazement, Peggotty burst from a hedge and climb into the cart. She took me in both her arms and squeezed me until the pressure on my nose was extremely painful, though I never thought of that till afterwards, when I found it very tender. Not a single word did Peggotty speak, releasing one of her arms, she put it down in her pocket to the elbow, and brought out some paper-bags of cakes, which she crammed into my pockets, and a purse which she put into my hand, but not one word did she say. After another and a final squeeze with both arms, she got down from the cart and ran away; and my belief is, and has always been, without a solitary button on her gown. I picked up one, of several that was rolling about, and treasured it as a keepsake for a long time.

The carrier looked at me, as if to inquire if she were coming back. I shook my head, and said I thought not. "Then come up!" said the carrier to the lazy horse, who came up accordingly.

Having by this time cried as much as I possibly could, I began to think it was of no use crying any more. The carrier seeing me in this resolution, proposed that my pocket handkerchief should be spread upon the horse's back to dry. I thanked him and agreed; and particularly small it looked under those circumstances.

I had now time to examine the purse. It was a stiff leather purse, with a snap, and had three bright shillings in it, which Peggotty had evidently polished up with whitening, for my greater delight. But its precious contents were two half-crowns folded together in a bit of paper, on which was written, in my mother's hand, "For Davy. With my love." I was so overcome by this, that I asked the carrier to be so good as reach me my pocket handkerchief again, but he said he thought I had better do without it; and I thought I really had; so I wiped my eyes on my sleeve and stopped myself.

For good, too; though, in consequence of my previous feelings, I was still occasionally seized with a stormy sob. After we had jogged on for some little time, I asked the carrier if he was going all the way.

"All the way where?" inquired the carrier.

"There," I said.

"Where's there?" inquired the carrier.

"Near London," I said.

"Why, that horse," said the carrier, jerking the rein to point him out, "would be deader than pork afore he got over half the ground."

"Are you only going to Yarmouth then?" I asked.

"That's about it," said the carrier. "And there I shall take you to the stage-cutch, and the stage-cutch that'll take you to—wherever it is."

I shared my cakes with the carrier, who asked if Peggotty made them, and told him yes, she did all our cooking. The carrier looked thoughtful, and then asked if I would send a message to Peggotty from him. I agreed, and the message was "Barkis is willing." While I was waiting for the coach at Yarmouth, I wrote to Peggotty:

"My dear Peggotty:—I have come here safe. Barkis is willing. My love to mamma. Yours affectionately.

"P.S.—He says he particularly wanted you to know *Barkis is willing*."

At Yarmouth I found dinner was ordered for me, and felt very shy at having a table all to myself, and very much alarmed when the waiter told me he had seen a gentleman fall down dead after drinking some of their beer. I said I would have some water, and was quite grateful to the waiter for drinking the ale that had been ordered for me, for fear the people of the hotel should be offended. He also helped me to eat my dinner, and accepted one of my bright shillings.

After a long, tiring journey by the coach, for there were no trains in those days, I arrived in London and was taken to the school at Blackheath, by one of the masters, Mr. Mell.

I gazed upon the schoolroom into which he took me, as the most forlorn and desolate place I had ever seen. I see it now. A long room, with three long rows of desks, and six of long seats, bristling all round with pegs for hats and slates. Scraps of old copy-books and exercises litter the dirty floor.

Mr. Mell having left me for a few moments, I went softly to the upper end of the room, observing all this as I crept along. Suddenly I came upon a pasteboard placard, beautifully written which was lying on the desk, and bore these words—*"Take care of him. He bites."*

I got upon the desk immediately, afraid of at least a great dog underneath. But, though I looked all round with anxious eyes, I could see nothing of him. I was still engaged in peering about when Mr. Mell came back, and asked me what I did up there.

"I beg your pardon, sir," says I, "if you please, I'm looking for the dog."

"Dog?" says he. "What dog?"

"Isn't it a dog, sir?"

"Isn't what a dog?"

"That's to be taken care of, sir; that bites."

"No, Copperfield," says he, gravely, "that's not a dog. That's a boy. My instructions are, Copperfield, to put this placard on your back. I am sorry to make such a beginning with you, but I must do it."

With that, he took me down, and tied the placard, which was neatly constructed for the purpose, on my shoulders like a knapsack; and wherever I went, afterwards, I had the consolation of carrying it.

What I suffered from that placard, nobody can imagine. Whether it was possible for people to see me or not, I always fancied that somebody was reading it. It was no relief to turn round and find nobody; for wherever my back was, there I imagined somebody always to be.

There was an old door in this playground, on which the boys had a custom of carving their names. It was completely covered with such inscriptions. In my dread of the end of the vacation and their coming back, I could not read one boy's name, without inquiring in what tone and with what emphasis *he* would read, "Take care of him. He bites." There was one boy—a certain J. Steerforth—who cut his name very deep and very often, who, I conceived, would read it in a rather strong voice, and afterwards pull my hair. There was another boy, one Tommy Traddles, who I dreaded would make game of it, and pretend to be dreadfully frightened of me. There was a third, George Demple, who I fancied would sing it. I have looked, a little shrinking creature, at that door, until the owners of all the names—there were five-and-forty of them in the school then, Mr. Mell said—seemed to cry out, each in his own way, "Take care of him. He bites!"

Tommy Traddles was the first boy who returned. He introduced himself by informing me that I should find his name on the right-hand corner of the gate, over the top bolt; upon that I said, "Traddles?" to which he replied, "The same," and then he asked me for a full account of myself and family.

It was fortunate for me that Traddles came back first. He enjoyed my placard so much that he saved me from the embarrassment of either telling about it or trying to hide it by presenting me to every other boy who came back, great or small, immediately on his arrival, in this form of introduction, "Look here! Here's a game!" Happily, too, the greater part of the boys came back low-spirited, and were not so boisterous at my expense as I had expected. Some of them certainly could not resist the temptation of pretending that I was a dog, and patting and smoothing me lest I should bite, and saying, "Lie down, sir!" and calling me Towzer. This was naturally confusing, among so many strangers, and cost some tears, but on the whole it was much better than I had anticipated.

I was not considered as being formally received into the school, however, until J. Steerforth arrived. Before this boy, who was reputed to be a great scholar, and was very good-looking, and at least half-a-dozen years older than I, I was carried as before a judge. He inquired, under a shed in the playground, into the particulars of my punishment, and was pleased to express his opinion that it was a "jolly shame;" for which I became bound to him ever afterwards.

"What money have you got, Copperfield?" he said, walking aside with me when he had disposed of my affair in these terms.

I told him seven shillings.

"You had better give it to me to take care of," he said. "At least, you can, if you like. You needn't if you don't like."

I hastened to comply with his friendly suggestion, and, opening Peggotty's purse, turned it upside down into his hand.

"Do you want to spend anything now?" he asked me.

"No, thank you," I replied.

"You can, if you like, you know," said Steerforth. "Say the word."

"No, thank you, sir," I repeated.

"Perhaps you'd like to spend a couple of shillings or so in a bottle of currant wine by-and-by, up in the bedroom?" said Steerforth. "You belong to my bedroom, I find."

It certainly had not occurred to me before, but I said, Yes, I should like that.

"Very good," said Steerforth. "You'll be glad to spend another shilling or so in almond cakes, I dare say?"

I said, "Yes, I should like that, too."

"And another shilling or so in biscuits, and another in fruit, eh?" said Steerforth. "I say, young Copperfield, you're going it!"

I smiled because he smiled, but I was a little troubled in my mind, too.

"Well!" said Steerforth. "We must make it stretch as far as we can; that's all. I'll do the best in my power for you. I can go out when

I like, and I'll smuggle the prog in." With these words he put the money in his pocket, and kindly told me not to make myself uneasy; he would take care it should be all right.

He was as good as his word, if that were all right which I had a secret misgiving was nearly all wrong—for I feared it was a waste of my mother's two half-crowns—though I had preserved the piece of paper they were wrapped in; which was a precious saving. When we went up-stairs to bed, he produced the whole seven shillings worth, and laid it out on my bed in the moonlight, saying:

"There you are, young Copperfield, and a royal spread you've got!"

I couldn't think of doing the honors of the feast at my time of life, while he was by; my hand shook at the very thought of it. I begged him to do me the favor of taking charge of the treat; and my request being seconded by the other boys who were in that room, he agreed to it, and sat upon my pillow, handing round the food—with perfect fairness, I must say—and giving out the currant wine in a little glass without a foot, which was his own property. As to me, I sat on his left hand, and the rest were grouped about us, on the nearest beds and on the floor.

How well I recollect our sitting there, talking in whispers; or their talking, and my respectfully listening, I ought rather to say; the moonlight falling a little way into the room, through the window, painting a pale window on the floor, and the greater part of us in shadow, except when Steerforth scratched a match, when he wanted to look for anything on the board, and shed a blue glare over us that was gone directly! A certain mysterious feeling, consequent on the darkness, the secrecy of the revel, and the whisper in which every-thing was said, steals over me again, and I listen to all they tell me, with a vague feeling of solemnity and awe, which makes me glad they are all so near, and frightens me (though I feign to laugh) when Traddles pretends to see a ghost in the corner.

I heard all kinds of things about the school and all belonging to it. I heard that Mr. Creakle was the sternest and most severe of masters; that he laid about him, right and left, every day of his life, charging in among the boys like a trooper, and slashing away, un-mercifully.

I heard that the man with the wooden leg, whose name was Tungay, was an obstinate fellow who had formerly been in the hop business, but had come into the line with Mr. Creakle, in consequence, as was supposed among the boys, of his having broken his leg in Mr. Creakle's service, and having done a deal of dishonest work for him, and knowing his secrets.

But the greatest wonder that I heard of Mr. Creakle was, there being one boy in the school on whom he never ventured to lay a hand, and that that boy being J. Steerforth. Steerforth himself confirmed this when it was stated, and said that he should like to begin to see him do it. On being asked by a mild boy (not me) how he would proceed if he did begin to see him do it, he scratched a match on purpose to shed a glare over his reply, and said he would commence with knocking him down with a blow on the forehead from the seven-and-six-penny ink-bottle that was always on the mantelpiece. We sat in the dark for some time, breathless.

I heard that Miss Creakle was regarded by the school in general as being in love with Steerforth; and I am sure, as I sat in the dark, thinking of his nice voice, and his fine face, and his easy manner, and his curling hair, I thought it very likely. I heard that Mr. Mell was not a bad sort of fellow, but hadn't a sixpence to bless himself with; and that there was no doubt that old Mrs. Mell, his mother, was as poor as Job.

One day, Traddles (the most unfortunate boy in the world) breaks a window accidentally with a ball. I shudder at this moment with the tremendous sensation of seeing it done, and feeling that the ball has bounded on to Mr. Creakle's sacred head.

Poor Traddles! In a tight sky-blue suit that made his arms and legs like German sausages, or roly-poly puddings, he was the merriest and most miserable of all the boys. He was always being caned—I think he was caned every day that half-year, except one holiday Monday, when he was only rulered on both hands—and was always going to write to his uncle about it, and never did. After laying his head on the desk for a little while, he would cheer up somehow, begin to laugh again, and draw skeletons all over his slate before his eyes were dry. I used at first to wonder what comfort Traddles found in drawing skeletons. But I believe he only did it because they were easy, and didn't want any features.

He was very honorable, Traddles was; and held it as a solemn duty in the boys to stand by one another. He suffered for this on several occasions; and particularly once, when Steerforth laughed in church, and the beadle thought it was Traddles, and took him out. I see him now, going away under guard, despised by the congregation. He never said who was the real offender, though he smarted for it next day, and was imprisoned so many hours that he came forth with a whole churchyard full of skeletons swarming all over his Latin Dictionary. But he had his reward. Steerforth said there was nothing of the sneak in Traddles, and we all felt that to be the highest praise. For my part, I could have gone through a great deal (though I was much less brave than Traddles, and nothing like so old) to have won such a reward, as praise from J. Steerforth.

To see Steerforth walk to church before us, arm-in-arm with Miss Creakle, was one of the great sights of my life. I didn't think Miss Creakle equal to little Em'ly in point of beauty, and I didn't love her (I didn't dare); but I thought her a young lady of extraordinary attractions, and in point of gentility not to be surpassed. When Steerforth, in white trousers, carried her parasol for her, I felt proud to know him; and believed that she could not choose but adore him with all her heart. Mr. Sharp and Mr. Mell were both great personages in my eyes; but Steerforth was to them what the sun was to two stars. An accidental matter strengthened the friendship between Steerforth and me, in a manner that inspired me with great pride and satisfaction, though it sometimes led to inconvenience. It happened on one occasion, when he was doing me the honor of talking to me in the playground that I remarked that something or somebody—I forget what now—was like something or somebody in the story of Peregrine Pickle. He said nothing at the time; but when I was going to bed at night, asked me if I had got that book.

I told him no, and explained how it was that I had read it, and all those other books of which I had made mention.

"And do you recollect them?" Steerforth said.

"Oh yes," I replied; I had a good memory, and I believed I recollected them very well.

"Then I tell you what, young Copperfield," said Steerforth, "you shall tell 'em to me. I can't get to sleep very early at night, and I generally wake rather early in the morning. We'll go over 'em one after another. We'll make some regular Arabian Nights of it."

I felt extremely flattered by this arrangement, and we commenced carrying out the plan that very evening.

Steerforth showed his thought for me in one particular instance, in an unflinching manner that was a little troublesome, to poor Traddles and the rest. Peggotty's promised letter—what a comfortable letter it was!—arrived before "the half" of the school-term was many weeks old; and with it a cake in a perfect nest of oranges, and two bottles of cowslip wine. This treasure, as in duty bound, I laid at the feet of Steerforth, and begged him to divide it among the boys.

"Now, I'll tell you what, young Copperfield," said he, "the wine shall be kept to wet your whistle when you are story-telling."

I blushed at the idea, and begged him, in my modesty, not to think of it. But he said he had observed I was sometimes hoarse—a little roopy was his exact expression—and it should be, every drop, set apart to the purpose he had mentioned. Accordingly, it was locked up in his box, and drawn off by himself in a phial, and administered to me through a piece of quill in the cork, when I was supposed to be in want of something to restore my voice. Sometimes, to make it more powerful, he was so kind as to squeeze orange juice into it, or to stir it up with ginger, or dissolve a peppermint drop in it.

We seem to me to have been months over Peregrine, and months more over the other stories. The school never flagged for want of a story, I am certain; and the wine lasted out almost as well as the matter. Poor Traddles—I never think of that boy but with a strange disposition to laugh, and with tears in my eyes—was a sort of echo to the story; and pretended to be overcome with laughing at the funny parts, and to be overcome with fear when there was any passage of an alarming character in the story. This rather put me out very often. It was a great jest of his, I recollect, to pretend that he couldn't keep his teeth from chattering, whenever mention was made of an Alguazil in connection with the adventures of Gil Blas; and I remember when Gil Blas met the captain of the robbers in Madrid, this unlucky joker acted such a shudder of terror that he was overheard by Mr. Creakle, who was prowling about the passage, and handsomely flogged for disorderly conduct in the bedroom.

One day I had a visit from Mr. Peggotty and Ham, who had brought two enormous lobsters, a huge crab, and a large canvas bag of shrimps, as they "remembered I was partial to a relish with my meals."

I was proud to introduce my friend Steerforth to these kind, simple friends, and told them how good Steerforth was to me, and how he helped me with my work and took care of me, and Steerforth delighted the fishermen with his friendly, pleasant manners.

The "relish" was greatly enjoyed by the boys at supper that night. Only poor Traddles became very ill from eating crab so late.

At last the holidays came, and I went home. The carrier, Barkis, met me at Yarmouth, and was rather gruff, which I soon found out was because he had not had any answer to his message. I promised to ask Peggotty for one.

Ah, what a strange feeling it was to be going home when it was not home, and to find that every object I looked at reminded me of the happy old home, which was like a dream I could never dream again!

God knows how like a child the memory may have been that was awakened within me by the sound of my mother's voice in the old parlor, when I set foot in the hall.

I believed, from the solitary and thoughtful way in which my mother murmured her song, that she was alone. And I went softly into the room. She was sitting by the fire, nursing an infant, whose tiny hand she held against her neck. Her eyes were looking down upon its face, and she sat singing to it. I was so far right, that she had no other companion.

I spoke to her, and she started, and cried out. But seeing me, she called me her dear Davy, her own boy; and, coming half across the room to meet me, kneeled down upon the ground and kissed me, and laid my head down on her bosom near the little creature that was nestling there, and put its hand up to my lips.

I wish I had died. I wish I had died then, with that feeling in my heart! I should have been more fit for heaven than I ever have been since.

"He is your brother," said my mother, fondling me. "Davy, my pretty boy: my poor child!" Then she kissed me more and more, and clasped me round the neck. This she was doing when Peggotty came running in, and bounced down on the ground beside us and went mad about us both for a quarter of an hour.

We had a very happy afternoon the day I came. Mr. and Miss Murdstone were out, and I sat with my mother and Peggotty, and told them all about my school and Steerforth, and took the little baby in my arms and nursed it lovingly. But when the Murdstones came back I was more unhappy than ever.

I felt uncomfortable about going down to breakfast in The morning, as I had never set eyes on Mr. Murdstone since the day when I committed my memorable offense. However, as it must be done, I went down, after two or three false starts halfway, and as many runs back on tiptoe to my own room, and presented myself in the parlor.

He was standing before the fire with his back to it, while Miss Murdstone made the tea. He looked at me steadily as I entered, but made no sign of recognition whatever.

I went up to him, after a moment of confusion, and said, "I beg your pardon, sir. I am very sorry for what I did, and I hope you will forgive me."

"I am glad to hear you are sorry, David," he replied.

"How do you do, ma'am?" I said to Miss Murdstone.

"Ah, dear me!" sighed Miss Murdstone, giving me the tea-caddy scoop instead of her finger. "How long are the holidays?"

"A month, ma'am."

"Counting from when?"

"From to-day, ma'am."

"Oh!" said Miss Murdstone. "Then here's *one* day off."

She kept a calendar of the holidays in this way, and every morning checked a day off in exactly the same manner. She did it gloomily until she came to ten, but when she got into two figures she became more hopeful, and, as the time advanced, even jocular.

Thus the holidays lagged away, until the morning came when Miss Murdstone said: "Here's the last day off!" and gave me the closing cup of tea of the vacation.

I was not sorry to go. Again Mr. Barkis appeared at the gate, and again Miss Murdstone in her warning voice said: "Clara!" when my mother bent over me, to bid me farewell.

I kissed her and my baby brother; it is not so much the embrace she gave me that lives in my mind, though it was as fervent as could be, as what followed the embrace.

I was in the carrier's cart when I heard her calling to me. I looked out, and she stood at the garden gate alone, holding her baby up in her arms for me to see. It was cold, still weather; and not a hair of her head, or fold of her dress, was stirred, as she looked intently at me, holding up her child.

So I lost her. So I saw her afterwards in my sleep at school—a silent presence near my bed—looking at me with the same intent face—holding up her baby in her arms.

About two months after I had been back at school I was sent for one day to go into the parlor. I hurried in joyfully, for it was my birthday, and I thought it might be a box from Peggotty—but, alas! no; it was very sad news Mrs. Creakle had to give me—my dear mamma had died! Mrs. Creakle was very kind and gentle to me, and the boys, especially Traddles, were very sorry for me.

I went home the next day, and heard that the dear baby had died too. Peggotty received me with great tenderness, and told me about my mother's illness and how she had sent a loving message to me.

"Tell my dearest boy that his mother, as she lay here, blessed him not once, but a thousand times," and she had prayed to God to protect and keep her fatherless boy.

Mr. Murdstone did not take any notice of me, nor had Miss Murdstone a word of kindness for me. Peggotty was to leave in a month, and, to my great joy, I was allowed to go with her on a visit to Mr. Peggotty. On our way I found out that the mysterious message I had given to Peggotty meant that Barkis wanted to marry her, and Peggotty had consented. Everyone in Mr. Peggotty's cottage was pleased to see me, and did their best to comfort me. Little Em'ly was at school when I arrived, and I went out to meet her. I knew the way by which she would come, and presently found myself strolling along the path to meet her.

A figure appeared in the distance before long, and I soon knew it to be Em'ly, who was a little creature still in stature, though she was grown. But when she drew nearer, and I saw her blue eyes looking bluer, and her dimpled face looking brighter, and her own self prettier and gayer, a curious feeling came over me that made me pretend not to know her, and pass by as if I were looking at something a long way off. I have done such a thing since in later life, or I am mistaken.

Little Em'ly didn't care a bit. She saw me well enough; but instead of turning round and calling after me, ran away laughing. This obliged me to run after her, and she ran so fast that we were very near the cottage before I caught her.

"Oh, it's you, is it?" said little Em'ly.

"Why, you knew who it was, Em'ly," said I.

"And didn't *you* know who it was?" said Em'ly. I was going to kiss her, but she covered her cherry lips with her hands, and said she wasn't a baby now, and ran away, laughing more than ever, into the house.

She seemed to delight in teasing me, which was a change in her I wondered at very much. The tea-table was ready, and our little locker was put out in its old place, but instead of coming to sit by me, she went and bestowed her company upon that grumbling Mrs. Gummidge; and on Mr. Peggotty's inquiring why, rumpled her hair all over her face to hide it, and would do nothing but laugh.

"A little puss it is!" said Mr. Peggotty, patting her with his great hand.

"Ah," said Peggotty, running his fingers through her bright curls, "here's another orphan, you see, sir, and here," giving Ham a back-handed knock in the chest, "is another of 'em, though he don't look much like it."

"If I had *you* for a guardian, Mr. Peggotty," said I, "I don't think I should *feel* much like it."

Em'ly was confused by our all observing her, and hung down her head, and her face was covered with blushes. Glancing up presently through her stray curls, and seeing that we were all looking at her still (I am sure I, for one, could have looked at her for hours), she ran away, and kept away till it was nearly bedtime.

I lay down in the old little bed in the stern of the boat, and the wind came moaning on across the flat as it had done before. But I could not help fancying, now that it moaned, of those who were gone; and instead of thinking that the sea might rise in the night and float the boat away, I thought of the sea that had risen, since I last heard those sounds, and drowned my happy home, I recollect, as the wind and water began to sound fainter in my ears, putting a short clause into my prayers, petitioning that I might grow up to marry little Em'ly, and so dropping lovingly asleep.

During this visit Peggotty was married to Mr. Barkis, and had a nice little house of her own, and I spent the night before I was to return home in a little room in the roof.

"Young or old, Davy dear, so long as I have this house over my head," said Peggotty, "you shall find it as if I expected you here directly every minute. I shall keep it as I used to keep your old little room, my darling, and if you was to go to China, you might think of its being kept just the same all the time you were away."

I felt how good and true a friend she was, and thanked her as well as I could, for they had brought me to the gate of my home, and Peggotty had me clasped in her arms.

I was poor and lonely at home, with no one near to speak a loving word, or a face to look on with love or liking, only the two persons who had broken my mother's heart. How utterly wretched and forlorn I felt! I found I was not to go back to school any more, and wandered about sad and solitary, neglected and uncared for. Peggotty's weekly visits were my only comfort. I longed to go to school, however hard an one, to be taught something anyhow, anywhere—but no one took any pains with me, and I had no friends near who could help me.

At last one day, after some weary months had passed, Mr. Murdstone told me I was to go to London and earn my own living. There was a place for me at Murdstone & Grinby's, a firm in the wine trade. My lodging and clothes would be provided for me by my step-father, and I would earn enough for my food and pocket money. The next day, I was sent up to London with the manager, dressed in a shabby little white hat with black crape round it for my mother, a black jacket, and hard, stiff corduroy trousers, a little fellow of ten years old, to fight my own battles with the world!

My place, I found, was one of the lowest in the firm of Murdstone & Grinby, with boys of no education and in quite an inferior station to myself—my duties were to wash the bottles, stick on labels, and so on. I was utterly miserable at being degraded in this way, when I thought of my former companions, Steerforth and Traddles, and my hopes of becoming a learned and famous man, and shed bitter tears, as I feared I would forget all I had learnt at school. My lodging, one bare little room, was in the house of some people named Micawber, shiftless, careless, good-natured people, who were always in debt and difficulties. I felt great pity for their misfortunes and did what I could to help poor Mrs. Micawber to sell her books and other little things she could spare, to buy food for herself, her husband, and their four children. I was too young and childish to know how to provide properly for myself, and often found I was obliged to live on bread and slices of cold pudding at the end of the week. If I had not been a very innocent-minded, good little boy, I might easily have fallen into bad ways at this time. But God took care of me and kept me from harm. I would not even tell Peggotty how miserable I was, for fear of distressing her.

The troubles of the Micawbers increased more and more, until at last they were obliged to leave London. I was very sad at this, for I had been with them so long that I felt they were my friends, and the prospect of being once more utterly alone and having to find a lodging with strangers, made me so unhappy that I determined to endure this sort of life no longer. The last Sunday the Micawbers were in town I dined with them. I had bought a spotted horse for their little boy and a doll for the little girl, and had saved up a shilling for the poor servant-girl. After I had seen them off the next morning by the coach, I wrote to Peggotty to ask her if she knew where my aunt, Miss Betsy Trotwood, lived, and to borrow half-a-guinea; for I had resolved to run away from Murdstone & Grinby's, and go to this aunt and tell her my story. I remembered my mother telling me of her visit when I was a baby, and that she fancied Miss Betsy had stroked her hair gently, and this gave me courage to appeal to her. Peggotty wrote, enclosing the half-guinea, and saying she only knew Miss Trotwood lived near Dover, but whether in that place itself, or at Folkestone, Sandgate, or Hythe, she could not tell. Hearing that all these places were close together, I made up my mind to start. As I had received my week's wages in advance, I waited till the following Saturday, thinking it would not be honest to go before. I went out to look for someone to carry my box to the coach office, and unfortunately hired a wicked young man who not only ran off with the box, but robbed me of my half-guinea, leaving me in dire distress. In despair, I started off to walk to Dover, and was forced to sell my waistcoat to buy some bread. The first night I found my way to my old school at Blackheath, and slept on a haystack close by, feeling some comfort in the thought of the boys being near. I knew Steerforth had left, or I would have tried to see him.

On I trudged the next day and sold my jacket at Chatham to a dreadful old man, who kept me waiting all day for the money, which was only one shilling and fourpence. I was afraid to buy anything but bread or to spend any money on a bed or a shelter for the night, and was terribly frightened by some rough tramps, who threw stones at me when I did not answer to their calls. After six days, I arrived at Dover, ragged, dusty, and half-dead with hunger and fatigue. But here, at first, I could get no tidings of my aunt, and, in despair, was going to try some of the other places Peggotty had mentioned, when the driver of a fly dropped his horsecloth, and as I was handing it up to him, I saw something kind in the man's face that encouraged me to ask once more if he knew where Miss Trotwood lived.

The man directed me towards some houses on the heights, and thither I toiled. Going into a little shop, I by chance met with Miss Trotwood's maid, who showed me the house, and went in leaving me standing at the gate, a forlorn little creature, without a jacket or waistcoat, my white hat crushed out of shape, my shoes worn out, my shirt and trousers torn and stained, my pretty curly hair tangled, my face and hands sunburnt and covered with dust. Lifting my eyes to one of the windows above, I saw a pleasant-faced gentleman with gray hair, who nodded at me several times, then shook his head and went away. I was just turning away to think what I should do, when a tall, erect elderly lady, with a gardening apron on and a knife in her hand, came out of the house, and began to dig up a root in the garden.

"Go away," she said. "Go away. No boys here."

But I felt desperate. Going in softly, I stood beside her, and touched her with my finger, and said timidly, "If you please, ma'am—" and when she looked up, I went on—

"Please, aunt, I am your nephew."

"Oh, Lord!" she exclaimed in astonishment, and sat flat down on the path, staring at me, while I went on—

"I am David Copperfield of Blunderstone, in Suffolk, where you came the night I was born, and saw my dear mamma. I have been very unhappy since she died. I have been neglected and taught nothing, and thrown upon myself, and put to work not fit for me. It made me run away to you. I was robbed at first starting out and have walked all the way, and have never slept in a bed since I began the journey." Here I broke into a passion of crying, and my aunt jumped up and took me into the house, where she opened a cupboard and took out some bottles, pouring some of the contents of each into my mouth, not noticing in her agitation what they were, for I fancied I tasted anise-seed water, anchovy sauce, and salad dressing! Then she put me on the sofa and sent the servant to ask "Mr. Dick" to come down. The gentleman whom I had seen at the window came in and was told by Miss Trotwood who the ragged little object on the sofa was, and she finished by saying—

"Now here you see young David Copperfield, and the question is what shall I do with him?"

"Do with him?" answered Mr. Dick. Then, after some consideration, and looking at me, he said, "Well, if I was you, I should wash him!"

Miss Trotwood was quite pleased at this, and a warm bath was got ready at once, after which I was dressed in a shirt and trousers belonging to Mr. Dick (for Janet had burnt my rags), rolled up in several shawls, and put on the sofa till dinner-time, where I slept, and woke with the impression that my aunt had come and put my hair off my face, and murmured, "Pretty fellow, poor fellow."

After dinner I had to tell my story all over again to my aunt and Mr. Dick. Miss Trotwood again asked Mr. Dick's advice, and was delighted when that gentleman suggested I should be put to bed. I knelt down to say my prayers that night in a pleasant room facing the sea, and as I lay in the clean, snow-white bed, I felt so grateful and comforted that I prayed earnestly I might never be homeless again, and might never forget the homeless.

The next morning my aunt told me she had written to Mr. Murdstone. I was alarmed to think that my step-father knew where I was, and exclaimed—

"Oh, I don't know what I shall do if I have to go back to Mr. Murdstone!"

But my aunt said nothing of her intentions, and I was uncertain what was to become of me. I hoped she might befriend me.

At last Mr. and Miss Murdstone arrived. To Miss Betsy's great indignation, Miss Murdstone rode a donkey across the green in front of the house, and stopped at the gate. Nothing made Miss Trotwood so angry as to see donkeys on that green, and I had already seen several battles between my aunt or Janet and the donkey boys.

After driving away the donkey and the boy who had dared to bring it there, Miss Trotwood received her visitors. She kept me near her, fenced in with a chair.

Mr. Murdstone told Miss Betsy that I was a very bad, stubborn, violent-tempered boy, whom he had tried to improve, but could not succeed; that he had put me in a respectable business from which I had run away. If Miss Trotwood chose to protect and encourage me now, she must do it always, for he had come to fetch me away from there and then, and if I was ready to come, and Miss Trotwood did not wish to give me up to be dealt with exactly as Mr. Murdstone liked, he would cast me off for always, and have no more to do with me.

"Are you ready to go, David?" asked my aunt.

But I answered no, and begged and prayed her for my father's sake to befriend and protect me, for neither Mr. nor Miss Murdstone had ever liked me or been kind to me and had made my mamma, who always loved me dearly, very unhappy about me, and I had been very miserable.

"Mr. Dick," said Miss Trotwood, "what shall I do with this child?"

Mr. Dick considered. "Have him measured for a suit of clothes directly."

"Mr. Dick," said Miss Trotwood, "your common sense is invaluable."

Then she pulled me towards her, and said to Mr. Murdstone, "You can go when you like. I'll take my chance with the boy. If he's all you say he is I can at least do as much for him as you have done. But I don't believe a word of it."

Then she told Mr. Murdstone what she thought of the way he had treated me and my mother, which did not make that gentleman feel very comfortable, and finished by turning to Miss Murdstone and saying—

"Good-day to you, too, ma'am, and if I ever see you ride a donkey across my green again, as sure as you have a head upon your shoulders, I'll knock your bonnet off and tread upon it!"

This startled Miss Murdstone so much that she went off quite quietly with her brother, while I, overjoyed, threw my arms round my aunt's neck, and kissed and thanked her with great heartiness.

Some clothes were bought for me that same day and marked "Trotwood Copperfield," for my aunt wished to call me by her name.

Now I felt my troubles were over, and I began quite a new life, well cared for and kindly treated. I was sent to a very nice school in Canterbury, where my aunt left me with these words, which I never forgot:

"Trot, be a credit to yourself, to me, and Mr. Dick, and heaven be with you. Never be mean in anything, never be false, never be cruel. Avoid these three vices, Trot, and I shall always be hopeful of you?"

I did my best to show my gratitude to my dear aunt by studying hard, and trying to be all she could wish.

When you are older you can read how Little David Copperfield grew up to be a good, clever man, and met again all his old friends, and made many new ones.

Also, what became of Steerforth, Traddles, the Peggottys, little Em'ly, and the Micawbers.

VIII

Jenny Wren

WALKING into the city one holiday, a great many years ago, a gentleman ran up the steps of a tall house in the neighborhood of St. Mary Axe. The lower windows were those of a counting-house but the blinds, like those of the entire front of the house, were drawn down.

The gentleman knocked and rang several times before any one came, but at last an old man opened the door. "What were you up to that you did not hear me?" said Mr. Fledgeby irritably.

"I was taking the air at the top of the house, sir," said the old man meekly, "it being a holiday. What might you please to want, sir?"

"Seated on the Crystal Carpet Were Two Girls."

"Humph! Holiday indeed," grumbled his master, who was a toy merchant amongst other things. He then seated himself in the counting-house and gave the old man—a Jew and Riah by name—

directions about the dressing of some dolls about which he had come to speak, and, as he rose to go, exclaimed—

"By-the-by, how *do* you take the air? Do you stick your head out of a chimney-pot?"

"No, sir, I have made a little garden on the leads."

"Let's look it at," said Mr. Fledgeby.

"Sir, I have company there," returned Riah hesitating, "but will you please come up and see them?"

Mr. Fledgeby nodded, and, passing his master with a bow, the old man led the way up flight after flight of stairs, till they arrived at the house-top. Seated on a carpet, and leaning against a chimney-stack, were two girls bending over books. Some humble creepers were trained round the chimney-pots, and evergreens were placed round the roof, and a few more books, a basket of gaily colored scraps, and bits of tinsel, and another of common print stuff lay near. One of the girls rose on seeing that Riah had brought a visitor, but the other re-marked, "I'm the person of the house down-stairs, but I can't get up, whoever you are, because my back is bad and my legs are queer."

"This is my master," said Riah, speaking to the two girls, "and this," he added, turning to Mr. Fledgeby, "is Miss Jenny Wren; she lives in this house, and is a clever little dressmaker for little people. Her friend Lizzie," continued Riah, introducing the second girl. "They are good girls, both, and as busy as they are good; in spare moments they come up here and take to book learning."

"We are glad to come up here for rest, sir," said Lizzie, with a grateful look at the old Jew. "No one can tell the rest what this place is to us."

"Humph!" said Mr. Fledgeby, looking round, "Humph!" He was so much surprised that apparently he couldn't get beyond that word, and as he went down again the old chimney-pots in their black cowls seemed to turn round and look after him as if they were saying "Humph" too.

Lizzie, the elder of these two girls, was strong and handsome, but little Jenny Wren, whom she so loved and protected, was small and deformed, though she had a beautiful little face, and the longest and loveliest golden hair in the world, which fell about her like a cloak of shining curls, as though to hide the poor little mis-shapen figure.

The Jew Riah, as well as Lizzie, was always kind and gentle to Jenny Wren, who called him her godfather. She had a father, who shared her poor little rooms, whom she called her child; for he was a bad, drunken, worthless old man, and the poor girl had to care for him, and earn money to keep them both. She suffered a great deal, for the poor little bent back always ached sadly, and was often weary from constant work but it was only on rare occasions, when alone or with her friend Lizzie, who often brought her work and sat in Jenny's room, that the brave child ever complained of her hard lot. Sometimes the two girls Jenny helping herself along with a crutch, would go and walk about the fashionable streets, in order to note how the grand folks were dressed. As they walked along, Jenny would tell her friend of the fancies she had when sitting alone at her work. "I imagine birds till I can hear them sing," she said one day, "and flowers till I can smell them. And oh! the beautiful children that come to me in the early mornings! They are quite different to other children, not like me, never cold, or anxious, or tired, or hungry, never any pain; they come in numbers, in long bright slanting rows, all dressed in white, and with shiny heads. 'Who is this in pain?' they say, and they sweep around and about me, take me up in their arms, and I feel so light, and all the pain goes. I know when they are coming a long way off, by hearing them say, 'Who is this in pain?' and I answer, 'Oh my blessed children, it's poor me! have pity on me, and take me up and then the pain will go."

Lizzie sat stroking and brushing the beautiful hair, whilst the tired little dressmaker leant against her when they were at home again, and as she kissed her good-night, a miserable old man stumbled into the room. "How's my Jenny Wren, best of children?" he mumbled, as he shuffled unsteadily towards her, but Jenny pointed her small finger towards him, exclaiming—"Go along with you, you bad, wicked old child, you troublesome, wicked old thing, *I* know where you have been, *I* know your tricks and your manners." The wretched man began to whimper like a scolded child. "Slave, slave, slave, from morning to night," went on Jenny, still shaking her finger at him, "and all for this; ain't you ashamed of yourself, you disgraceful boy?"

"Yes; my dear, yes," stammered the tipsy old father, tumbling into a corner. Thus was the poor little dolls' dressmaker dragged down day by day by the very hands that should have cared for and held her up; poor, poor little dolls' dressmaker! One day when Jenny was on her way home with Riah, who had accompanied her on one of her walks to the West End, they came on a small crowd of people. A tipsy man had been knocked down and badly hurt. "Let us see what it is!" said Jenny, coming swiftly forward on her crutches. The next moment she exclaimed—"Oh, gentlemen—gentlemen, he is my child, he belongs to me, my poor, bad old child!"

"Your child—belongs to you," repeated the man who was about to lift the helpless figure on to a stretcher, which had been brought for the purpose. "Aye, it's old Dolls—tipsy old Dolls," cried someone in the crowd, for it was by this name that they knew the old man.

"He's her father, sir," said Riah in a low tone to the doctor who was now bending over the stretcher.

"So much the worse," answered the doctor, "for the man is dead."

Yes, "Mr. Dolls" was dead, and many were the dresses which the weary fingers of the sorrowful little worker must make in order to pay for his humble funeral and buy a black frock for herself. Riah sat by her in her poor room, saying a word of comfort now and then, and Lizzie came and went, and did all manner of little things to help her; but often the tears rolled down on to her work. "My poor child," she said to Riah, "my poor old child, and to think I scolded him so."

"You were always a good, brave, patient girl," returned Riah, smiling a little over her quaint fancy about her *child*, "always good and patient, however tired."

And so the poor little "person of the house" was left alone but for the faithful affection of the kind Jew and her friend Lizzie. Her room grew pretty and comfortable, for she was in great request in her "profession," as she called it, and there were now no one to spend and waste her earnings. But nothing could make her life otherwise than a suffering one till the happy morning when her child-angels visited her for the last time and carried her away to the land where all such pain as hers is healed for evermore.

IX

Pip's Adventure

"Keep Still, You Little Imp, or I'll Cut Your Throat."

ALL that little Philip Pirrip, usually called Pip, knew about his father and mother, and his five little brothers, was from seeing their tombstones in the churchyard. He was cared for by his sister, who was twenty years older than himself. She had married a blacksmith, named Joe Gargery, a kind, good man, while she, unfortunately, was a hard, stern woman, and treated her little brother and her amiable husband with great harshness. They lived in a marshy part of the country, about twenty miles from the sea.

One cold, raw day towards evening, when Pip was about six years old, he had wandered into the churchyard, and was trying to make out what he could of the inscriptions on his family tombstones. The darkness was coming on, and feeling very lonely and frightened, he began to cry.

"Hold your noise!" cried a terrible voice; and a man started up from among the graves close to him. "Keep still, you little imp, or I'll cut your throat!"

He was a dreadful looking man, dressed in coarse gray cloth, with a great iron on his leg. Wet, muddy, and miserable, he limped and shivered, and glared and growled; his teeth chattered in his head, as he seized Pip, by the chin.

"Oh! don't cut my throat, sir," cried Pip, in terror. "Pray don't do it, sir."

"Tell us your name!" said the man. "Quick!"

"Pip, sir."

"Once more," said the man, staring at him, "Give it mouth."

"Pip. Pip, sir."

"Show us where you live," said the man. "Point out the place."

Pip showed him the village, about a mile or more from the church.

The man looked at him for a moment, and then turned him upside down and emptied his pockets. He found nothing in them but a piece of bread, which he ate ravenously.

"You young dog," said the man, licking his lips, "what fat cheeks you ha' got. . . . Darn me if I couldn't eat 'em, and if I han't half a mind to!"

Pip said earnestly that he hoped he would not.

"Now lookee here," said the man. "Where's your mother?"

"There sir," said Pip.

At this the man started and seemed about to run away, but stopped and looked over his shoulder.

"There, sir," explained Pip, showing him the tombstone.

"Oh, and is that your father along of your mother?"

"Yes, sir," said Pip.

"Ha!" muttered the man, "then who d'ye live with—supposin' you're kindly let to live, which I han't made up my mind about?"

"My sister, sir, Mrs. Joe Gargery, wife of Joe Gargery, the blacksmith, sir."

"Blacksmith, eh?" said the man, and looked down at his leg. Then he seized the trembling little boy by both arms, and glaring down at him, he said—

"Now lookee here, the question being whether you're to be let to live. You know what a file is?"

"Yes, sir."

"And you know what wittles is. Something to eat?"

"Yes, sir."

"You get me a file, and you get me wittles—you bring 'em both to me." All this time he was tilting poor Pip backwards till he was so dreadfully frightened and giddy that he clung to the man with both hands.

"You bring me, to-morrow morning early, that file and them wittles. You do it, and you never dare to say a word or dare to make a sign concerning your having seen such a person as me, or any person sumever, and you shall be let to live." Then he threatened all sorts of dreadful and terrible things to poor Pip if he failed to do all he had commanded, and made him solemnly promise to bring him what he wanted, and to keep the secret. Then he let him go, saying, "You remember what you've undertook, and you get home."

"Goo—good-night, sir," faltered Pip.

"Much of that!" said he, glancing over the cold wet flat. "I wish I was a frog or a eel!"

Pip ran home without stopping. Joe was sitting in the chimney-corner, and told him Mrs. Joe had been out to look for him, and taken Tickler with her. Tickler was a cane, and Pip was rather down-hearted by this piece of news.

Mrs. Joe came in almost directly, and, after having given Pip a taste of Tickler, she sat down to prepare the tea, and, cutting a huge slice of bread and butter, she gave half of it to Joe and half to Pip. Pip managed, after some time, to slip his down the leg of his trousers, and Joe, thinking he had swallowed it, was dreadfully alarmed and begged him not to bolt his food like that. "Pip, old chap, you'll do yourself a mischief—it'll stick somewhere, you can't have chewed it, Pip. You know, Pip, you and me is always friends and I'd be the last one to tell upon you any time, but such a—such a most uncommon bolt as that."

"Been bolting his food, has he?" cried Mrs. Joe.

"You know, old chap," said Joe. "I bolted myself when I was your age—frequent—and as a boy I've been among a many bolters; but I never see your bolting equal yet, Pip, and it's a mercy you ain't bolted dead."

Mrs. Joe made a dive at Pip, fished him up by the hair, saying, "You come along and be dosed."

It was Christmas eve, and Pip had to stir the pudding from seven to eight, and found the bread and butter dreadfully in his way. At last he slipped out and put it away in his little bedroom.

Poor Pip passed a wretched night, thinking of the dreadful promise he had made, and as soon as it was beginning to get light outside he got up and crept down-stairs, fancying that every board creaked out "Stop thief!" and "Get up, Mrs. Joe!"

As quickly as he could, he took some bread, some rind of cheese, about half a jar of mince-meat, which he tied up in a handkerchief, with the slice of bread and butter, some brandy from a stone bottle, a meat-bone with very little on it, and a pork-pipe, which he found on an upper shelf. Then he got a file from among Joe's tools, and ran for the marshes.

It was a very misty morning, and Pip imagined that all the cattle stared at him, as if to say, "Halloa, young thief!" and one black ox with a white cravat on, that made Pip think of a clergyman, looked so accusingly at him, that Pip blubbered out, "I couldn't help it, sir! It wasn't for myself I took it."

Upon which the ox put down his head, blew a cloud of smoke out of his nose, and vanished with a kick-up of his hind legs and a flourish of his tail.

Pip was soon at the place of meeting after that, and there was the man—hugging himself and limping to and fro, as if he had never all night left off hugging and limping. He was awfully cold, to be sure. Pip half expected to see him drop down before his face and die of cold. His eyes looked so awfully hungry, too, that when Pip handed him the file it occurred to him he would have tried to eat it, if he had not seen the bundle. He did not turn Pip upside down, this time, to get at what he had, but left him right side upward while he opened the bundle and emptied his pockets.

"What's in the bottle, boy?" said he.

"Brandy," said Pip.

He was already handing mince-pie down his throat in the most curious manner, more like a man who was putting it away some-where in a violent hurry than a man who was eating it—but he left off to take some of the liquor, shivering all the while so violently that it was quite as much as he could do to keep the neck of the bottle between his teeth.

"I think you have got the chills," said Pip.

"I'm much of your opinion, boy," said he.

"It's bad about here. You've been lying out on the marshes, and they're dreadful for the chills. Rheumatic, too."

"I'll eat my breakfast before they're the death of me," said he. "I'd do that, if I was going to be strung up to that there gallows as there is over there directly arterward. I'll beat the shivers so far, I'll bet you a guinea."

He was gobbling mince-meat, meat-bone, bread, cheese, and pork-pie all at once, staring distrustfully while he did so at the mist all round, and often stopping—even stopping his jaws—to listen. Some real or fancied sound, some clink upon the river or breathing of beasts upon the marsh, now gave him a start, and he said, suddenly:

"You're not a false imp? You brought no one with you?"

"No, sir! No!"

"Nor told nobody to follow you?"

"No!"

"Well," said he, "I believe you. You'd be but a fierce young hound indeed, if at your time of life you should help to hunt a wretched warmint, hunted as near death and dunghill as this poor wretched warmint is!"

Something clicked in his throat, as if he had works in him like a clock, and was going to strike. And he smeared his ragged, rough sleeve over his eyes.

Pitying his desolation, and watching him as he gradually settled down upon the pie, Pip made bold to say, "I am glad you enjoy it."

"Did you speak?"

"I said I was glad you enjoyed it."

"Thankee, my boy—. I do."

Pip had often watched a large dog eating his food; and he now noticed a decided similarity between the dog's way of eating and the man's. The man took strong, sharp, sudden bites, just like the dog. He swallowed, or rather snapped up, every mouthful too soon and too fast; and he looked sideways here and there while he ate, as if he thought there was danger of somebody's coming to take the pie away. He was altogether too unsettled in his mind over it to enjoy it comfortably, Pip thought, or to have anybody to dine with him, without making a chop with his jaws at the visitor. In all of which particulars he was very like the dog.

Pip watched him trying to file the iron off his leg, and then being afraid of stopping longer away from home, he ran off.

Pip passed a wretched morning, expecting every moment that the disappearance of the pie would be found out. But Mrs. Joe was too much taken up with preparing the dinner, for they were expecting visitors, and were to have a superb dinner, consisting of a leg of pickled pork and greens, and a pair of roast stuffed fowls, a mince-pie, and a pudding.

Just at the end of the dinner Pip thought his time had come to be found out, for his sister said graciously to her guests—

"You must taste a most delightful and delicious present I have had. It's a pie, a savory pork-pie."

Pip could bear it no longer, and ran for the door, and there ran head foremost into a party of soldiers with their muskets, one of whom held out a pair of handcuffs to him, saying, "Here you are, look sharp, come on." But they had not come for him, they only wanted Joe to mend the handcuffs, for they were on the search for two convicts who had escaped and were somewhere hid in the marshes. This turned the attention of Mrs. Joe from the disappearance of the pie, without which she had come back, in great astonishment. When the handcuffs were mended the soldiers went off, accompanied by Joe and one of the visitors, and Joe took Pip and carried him on his back.

Pip whispered, "I hope, Joe, we shan't find them," and Joe answered, "I'd give a shilling if they had cut and run, Pip."

But the soldiers soon caught them, and one was the wretched man who had talked with Pip; and once when he looked at Pip, the child shook his head to try and let him know he had said nothing.

But the convict, without looking at anyone, told the sergeant he wanted to say something to prevent other people being under suspicion, and said he had taken some "wittles" from the blacksmith's. "It was some broken wittles, that's what it was, and a dram of liquor, and a pie."

"Have you happened to miss such an article as a pie, blacksmith?" inquired the sergeant.

"My wife did, at the very moment when you came in. Don't you know, Pip?"

"So," said the convict, looking at Joe, "you're the blacksmith, are you? Then, I'm sorry to say, I've eat your pie."

"God knows you're welcome to it," said Joe. "We don't know what you have done, but we wouldn't have you starved to death for it, poor miserable fellow-creature. Would us, Pip?"

Then the boat came, and the convicts were taken back to their prison, and Joe carried Pip home.

Some years after, some mysterious friend sent money for Pip to be educated and brought up as a gentleman; but it was only when Pip was quite grown up that he discovered this mysterious friend was the wretched convict who had frightened him so dreadfully that cold, dark Christmas eve. He had been sent to a far away land, and there had grown rich; but he never forgot the little boy who had been kind to him.

X

Todgers'

THIS is the story of a visit made by Mr. Pecksniff, a very pompous man, and his two daughters Miss Mercy and Miss Charity, to the boarding-house kept by Mrs. Todgers, in London; and a call while there on Miss Pinch, a governess or young lady teaching in a rich family.

Mr. Pecksniff with his two beautiful young daughters looked about him for a moment, and then knocked at the door of a very dingy building, even among the choice collection of dingy houses around, on the front of which was a little oval board, like a tea-tray, with this inscription—"Commercial Boarding-house: M. Todgers."

It seemed that M. Todgers was not up yet, for Mr. Pecksniff knocked twice and rang three times without making any impression on anything but a dog over the way. At last a chain and some bolts were withdrawn with a rusty noise, and a small boy with a large red head, and no nose to speak of, and a very dirty boot on his left arm, appeared; who (being surprised) rubbed the nose just mentioned with the back of a shoe-brush, and said nothing.

"Still abed, my man?" asked Mr. Pecksniff.

"Still abed!" replied the boy. "I wish they was still abed. They're very noisy abed; all calling for their boots at once. I thought you was the paper, and wondered why you didn't shove yourself through the grating as usual. What do you want?"

Considering his years, which were tender, the youth may be said to have asked this question sternly, and in something of a defiant manner. But Mr. Pecksniff, without taking offense at his bearing, put a card in his hand, and bade him take that up-stairs, and show them in the meanwhile into a room where there was a fire.

Surely there never was, in any other borough, city, or hamlet, in the world, such a singular sort of a place as Todgers'. And surely London, to judge from that part of it which hemmed Todgers' round, and hustled it, and crushed it, and stuck its brick-and-mortar elbows into it, and kept the air from it, and stood perpetually between it and the light, was worthy of Todgers'.

There were more trucks near Todgers' than you would suppose a whole city could ever need; not trucks at work but a vagabond race, forever lounging in the narrow lanes before their masters' doors and stopping up the pass; so that when a stray hackney-coach or lumbering wagon came that way, they were the cause of such an uproar as enlivened the whole neighborhood, and made the very bells in the next church-tower ring again. In the narrow dark streets near Todgers', wine-merchants and wholesale dealers in grocery-ware had perfect little towns of their own; and, deep among the very foundations of these buildings, the ground was undermined and burrowed out into stables, where cart-horses, troubled by rats, might be heard on a quiet Sunday, rattling their halters, as disturbed spirits in tales of haunted houses are said to clank their chains.

To tell of half the queer old taverns that had a drowsy and secret existence near Todgers' would fill a goodly book; while a second volume no less in size might be given to an account of the quaint old guests who frequented their dimly-lighted parlors.

The top of the house was worthy of notice. There was a sort of terrace on the roof, with posts and fragments of rotten lines, once intended to dry clothes upon; and there were two or three tea-chests out there, full of earth, with forgotten plants in them, like old walking-sticks. Whoever climbed to this observatory was stunned at first from having knocked his head against the little door in coming out; and, after that, was for the moment choked from having looked, perforce, straight down the kitchen chimney; but these two stages over, there were things to gaze at from the top of Todgers', well worth your seeing, too. For, first and foremost, if the day were bright, you observed upon the house-tops, stretching far away, a long dark path—the shadow of the tall Monument which stands in memory of the great fire in London many years before: and turning round, the Monument itself was close beside you, with every hair erect upon his golden head, as if the doings of the city frightened him. Then there were steeples, towers, belfries, shining vanes and masts of ships, a very forest. Gables, house-tops, garret-windows, wilderness upon wilderness. Smoke and noise enough for all the world at once.

After the first glance, there were slight features in the midst of this crowd of objects, which sprung out from the mass without any reason, as it were, and took hold of the attention whether the spectator would or no. Thus, the revolving chimney-pots on one great stack of buildings seemed to be turning gravely to each other every now and then, and whispering the result of their separate observation of what was going on below. Others, of a crooked-back shape, appeared to be maliciously holding themselves askew, that they might shut the prospect out and baffle Todgers'. The man who was mending a pen at an upper window over the way became of vast importance in the scene, and made a blank in it, ridiculously large in its size, when he went away. The fluttering of a piece of cloth upon the dyer's pole had far more interest for the moment than all the changing motion of the crowd. Yet even while the looker-on felt angry with himself for this, and wondered how it was the tumult swelled into a roar; the hosts of objects seemed to thicken and expand a hundredfold; and after gazing round him, quite scared, he turned into Todgers' again, much more rapidly than he came out; and ten to one he told M. Todgers afterwards that if he hadn't done so, he would certainly have come into the street by the shortest cut: that is to say, head-foremost.

So said the two Miss Pecksniffs, when they came down with Mrs. Todgers from the roof of the house; leaving the youthful porter to close the door and follow them down-stairs: who being of a playful temperament, and contemplating with a delight peculiar to his sex and time of life any chance of dashing himself into small fragments, lingered behind to walk upon the wall around the roof.

It was the second day of their stay in London, and by this time the Misses Pecksniff and Mrs. Todgers were becoming very friendly, insomuch that the last-named lady had already told the story of three early disappointments in love; and had furthermore given her young friends a general account of the life, conduct, and character of Mr. Todgers: who, it seemed, had cut his life as a husband rather short, by unlawfully running away from his happiness, and staying for a time in foreign countries as a bachelor.

"Your pa was once a little particular in his attentions, my dears," said Mrs. Todgers, "but to be your ma was too much happiness denied me. You'd hardly know who this was done for, perhaps?"

She called their attention to an oval miniature, like a little blister, which was tacked up over the kettle-holder, and in which there was a dreamy shadowing forth of her own visage.

"It's a speaking likeness!" cried the two Misses Pecksniff.

"It was considered so once," said Mrs. Todgers, warming herself in a gentlemanly manner at the fire: "but I hardly thought you would have known it, my loves."

They would have known it anywhere. If they could have met with it in the street or seen it in a shop-window, they would have cried, "Good gracious! Mrs. Todgers!"

"Being in charge of a boarding-house like this makes sad havoc with the features, my dear Misses Pecksniff," said Mrs. Todgers. "The gravy alone is enough to add twenty years to one's age, I do assure you."

"Lor!" cried the two Misses Pecksniff.

"The anxiety of that one thing, my dears," said Mrs. Todgers, "keeps the mind continually upon the stretch. There is no such passion in human nature as the passion for gravy among business men. It's nothing to say a joint won't yield—a whole animal wouldn't yield—the amount of gravy they expect each day at dinner. And what I have undergone in consequence," cried Mrs. Todgers, raising her eyes and shaking her head, "no one would believe!"

"Just like Mr. Pinch, Mercy!" said Charity. "We have always noticed it in him, you remember?"

"Yes, my dear," giggled Mercy, "but we have never given it him, you know."

Mr. Pecksniff kept what was called a school for architects, and Tom Pinch was one of his students.

"You, my dears, having to deal with your pa's pupils who can't help themselves, are able to take your own way," said Mrs. Todgers, "but in a boarding-house, where any gentleman may say, any Saturday evening, 'Mrs. Todgers, this day week we part, in consequence of the cheese,' it is not so easy to preserve a pleasant understanding. Your pa was kind enough," added the good lady, "to invite me to take a ride with you to-day; and I think he mentioned that you were going to call upon Miss Pinch. Any relation to the gentleman you were speaking of just now, Miss Pecksniff?"

"For goodness' sake, Mrs. Todgers," interposed the lively Mercy, "don't call him a gentleman. My dear Cherry, Pinch a gentleman! The idea!"

"What a wicked girl you are!" cried Mrs. Todgers, embracing her with great affection. "You are quite a joker, I do declare! My dear Miss Pecksniff, what a happiness your sister's spirits must be to your pa and self!"

"That Pinch is the most hideous, goggle-eyed creature, Mrs. Todgers, in existence," resumed Mercy: "quite an ogre. The ugliest, awkwardest, frightfullest being, you can imagine. This is his sister, so I leave you to suppose what *she* is. I shall be obliged to laugh outright, I know I shall!" cried the charming girl. "I never shall be able to keep my face straight. The notion of a Miss Pinch really living at all is sufficient to kill one, but to see her—oh my stars!"

Mrs. Todgers laughed immensely at the dear love's humor, and declared she was quite afraid of her, that she was. She was so very severe.

"Who is severe?" cried a voice at the door. "There is no such thing as severity in our family, I hope!" And then Mr. Pecksniff peeped smilingly into the room, and said, "May I come in, Mrs. Todgers?"

Mrs. Todgers almost screamed, for the little door between that room and the inner one being wide open, there was a full showing of the sofa-bedstead open as a bed, and not closed as a sofa. But she had the presence of mind to close it in the twinkling of an eye; and having done so, said, though not without confusion, "Oh yes, Mr. Pecksniff, you can come in if you please."

"How are we to-day," said Mr. Pecksniff, jocosely; "and what are our plans? Are we ready to go and see Tom Pinch's sister? Ha, ha, ha! Poor Thomas Pinch!"

"Are we ready," returned Mrs. Todgers, nodding her head in a mysterious manner, "to send a favorable reply to Mr. Jinkins' round-robin?[4] That's the first question, Mr. Pecksniff."

"Why Mr. Jinkins' robin, my dear madam?" asked Mr. Pecksniff, putting one arm round Mercy and the other round Mrs. Todgers, whom he seemed for the moment, to mistake for Charity. "Why Mr. Jinkins'?"

"Because he began to get it up, and indeed always takes the lead in the house," said Mrs. Todgers, playfully. "That's why, sir."

"Jinkins is a man of superior talents," observed Mr. Pecksniff. "I have formed a great regard for Jinkins. I take Jinkins' desire to pay polite attention to my daughters as an additional proof of the friendly feelings of Jinkins, Mrs. Todgers."

"Well now," returned the lady, "having said so much, you must say the rest, Mr. Pecksniff: so tell the dear young ladies all about it."

With these words, she gently drew away from Mr. Pecksniff's grasp, and took Miss Charity into her own embrace; though whether she was led to this act solely by the affection she had conceived for that young lady, or whether it had any reference to a lowering, not to say distinctly spiteful expression which had been visible in her face for some moments, has never been exactly ascertained. Be this as it may, Mr. Pecksniff went on to inform his daughters of the purpose and history of the round-robin aforesaid, which was, in brief, that the young men who helped to make up the sum and substance of that company, called Todgers', desired the honor of their presence at the general table so long as they remained in the house, and besought that they would grace the board at dinner-time next day, the same being Sunday. He further said that, Mrs. Todgers having consented to this invitation, he was willing, for his part, to accept it; and so left them that he might write his gracious answer, the while they armed themselves with their best bonnets for the utter defeat and overthrow of Miss Pinch.

Tom Pinch's sister was governess in a family, a lofty family; perhaps the wealthiest brass and copper founder's family known to

---

4.   A "round-robin" is a letter signed by all the people of a company, with the names written in a circle around the letter so that no name will be first or last.

mankind. They lived at Camberwell; in a house so big and fierce that its mere outside, like the outside of a giant's castle, struck terror into vulgar minds and made bold persons quail. There was a great front gate, with a great bell, whose handle was in itself a note of admiration; and a great lodge, which, being close to the house, rather spoiled the look-out certainly, but made the look-in tremendous. At this entry, a great porter kept constant watch and ward; and when he gave the visitor high leave to pass, he rang a second great bell, answering to whose notes a great footman appeared in due time at the great hall-door with such great tags upon his liveried shoulders that he was perpetually entangling and hooking himself among the chairs and tables and led a life of torment which could scarcely have been surpassed if he had been a blue-bottle in a world of cobwebs.

To this mansion, Mr. Pecksniff, accompanied by his daughters and Mrs. Todgers, drove gallantly in a one-horse fly. The foregoing ceremonies having been all performed, they were ushered into the house, and so, by degrees, they got at last into a small room with books in it, where Mr. Pinch's sister was at that moment instructing her eldest pupil: to wit, a little woman thirteen years old, who had already arrived at such a pitch of whalebone and education that she had nothing girlish about her; which was a source of great rejoicing to all her relations and friends.

"Visitors for Miss Pinch!" said the footman. He must have been an ingenious young man, for he said it very cleverly; with a nice distinction in his manner between the cold respect with which he would have announced visitors to the family and the warm personal interest with which he would have announced visitors to the cook.

"Visitors for Miss Pinch!"

Miss Pinch rose hastily with such tokens of agitation as plainly declared that her list of callers was not numerous. At the same time, the little pupil became alarmingly upright, and prepared herself to take notice of all that might be said and done. For the lady of the establishment was curious in the natural history and habits of the animal called Governess, and encouraged her daughters to report thereon whenever occasion served; which was, in reference to all parties concerned, very proper, improving, and pleasant.

It is a melancholy fact, but it must be related, that Mr. Pinch's sister was not at all ugly. On the contrary, she had a good face—a very mild and friendly face; and a pretty little figure—slight and short, but remarkable for its neatness. There was something of her brother, much of him indeed, in a certain gentleness of manner, and in her look of timid truthfulness; but she was so far from being a fright, or a dowdy, or a horror, or anything else predicted by the two Misses Pecksniff, that those young ladies naturally regarded her with great indignation, feeling that this was by no means what they had come to see.

Miss Mercy, as having the larger share of gayety, bore up the best against this disappointment, and carried it off, in outward show at least, with a titter; but her sister, not caring to hide her disdain, expressed it pretty openly in her looks. As to Mrs. Todgers, she leaned on Mr. Pecksniff's arm and preserved a kind of genteel grimness, suitable to any state of mind, and involving any shade of opinion.

"Don't be alarmed, Miss Pinch," said Mr. Pecksniff, taking her hand condescendingly in one of his, and patting it with the other. "I have called to see you, in pursuance of a promise given to your brother, Thomas Pinch. My name—compose yourself, Miss Pinch—is Pecksniff."

The good man spoke these words as though he would have said, "You see in me, young person, the friend of your race; the patron of your house; the preserver of your brother, who is fed with manna daily from my table; and in right of whom there is a considerable balance in my favor at present standing in the books beyond the sky. But I have no pride, for I can afford to do without it!"

The poor girl felt it all as if it had been Gospel Truth. Her brother, writing in the fullness of his simple heart, had often told her so, and how much more! As Mr. Pecksniff ceased to speak, she hung her head, and dropped a tear upon his hand.

"Oh, very well, Miss Pinch!" thought the sharp pupil, "crying before strangers as if you didn't like the situation!"

"Thomas is well," said Mr. Pecksniff; "and sends his love and this letter. I cannot say, poor fellow, that he will ever become great in our profession; but he has the will to do well, which is the next thing to having the power; and, therefore, we must bear with him. Eh?"

"I know he has the will, sir," said Tom Pinch's sister, "and I know how kindly and thoughtfully you cherish it, for which neither he nor I can ever be grateful enough, as we often say in writing to each other. The young ladies, too," she added, glancing gratefully at his two daughters. "I know how much we owe to them."

"My dears," said Mr. Pecksniff, turning to them with a smile: "Thomas' sister is saying something you will be glad to hear, I think."

"We can't take any merit to ourselves, papa!" cried Cherry, as they both showed Tom Pinch's sister, with a courtesy, that they would feel obliged if she would keep her distance. "Mr. Pinch's being so well provided for is owing to you alone, and we can only say how glad we are to hear that he is as grateful as he ought to be."

"Oh, very well, Miss Pinch!" thought the pupil again. "Got a grateful brother, living on other people's kindness!"

"It was very kind of you," said Tom Pinch's sister, with Tom's own simplicity and Tom's own smile, "to come here—very kind indeed: though how great a kindness you have done me in gratifying my wish to see you, and to thank you with my own lips, you, who make so light of benefits conferred, can scarcely think."

"Very grateful; very pleasant; very proper;" murmured Mr. Pecksniff.

"It makes me happy too," said Ruth Pinch, who, now that her first surprise was over, had a chatty, cheerful way with her, and a single-hearted desire to look upon the best side of everything, which was the very moral and image of Tom; "very happy to think that you will be able to tell him how more than comfortably I am situated here, and how unnecessary it is that he should ever waste a regret on my being cast upon my own resources. Dear me! So long as I heard that he was happy and he heard that I was," said Tom's sister, "we could both bear, without one impatient or complaining thought, a great deal more than ever we have had to endure, I am certain." And if ever the plain truth were spoken on this occasionally false earth, Tom's sister spoke it when she said that.

"Ah!" cried Mr. Pecksniff, whose eyes had in the meantime wandered to the pupil; "certainly. And how do *you* do, my very interesting child?"

"Quite well, I thank you, sir," replied that frosty innocent.

"A sweet face this, my dears," said Mr. Pecksniff, turning to his daughters. "A charming manner!"

Both young ladies had been in delight with the child of a wealthy house (through whom the nearest road and shortest cut to her parents might be supposed to lie) from the first. Mrs. Todgers vowed that anything one-quarter so angelic she had never seen. "She wanted but a pair of wings, a dear," said that good woman, "to be a young syrup"—meaning, possibly, young sylph or seraph.

"If you will give that to your distinguished parents, my amiable little friend," said Mr. Pecksniff, producing one of his professional cards, "and will say that I and my daughters——"

"And Mrs. Todgers, pa," said Mercy.

"And Mrs. Todgers, of London," added Mr. Pecksniff, "that I, and my daughters, and Mrs. Todgers, of London, did not intrude upon them, as our object simply was to take some notice of Miss Pinch, whose brother is a young man in my employment; but that I could not leave this very noble mansion without adding my humble tribute, as an architect, to the correctness and elegance of the owner's taste, and to his just appreciation of that beautiful art, to the cultivation of which I have devoted a life, and to the promotion of whose glory and advancement I have sacrificed a—a fortune—I shall be very much obliged to you."

"Missis' compliments to Miss Pinch," said the footman, suddenly appearing and speaking in exactly the same key as before, "and begs to know wot my young lady is a-learning of just now."

"Oh!" said Mr. Pecksniff, "here is the young man. *He* will take the card. With my compliments, if you please, young man. My dears, we are interrupting the studies. Let us go."

One evening, following the visit to Miss Pinch, there was a great bustle at Todgers', partly owing to some additional domestic preparations for the morrow and partly to the excitement always arising in that house from Saturday night, when every gentleman's linen arrived at a different hour in his own little bundle, with his private account pinned on the outside. Shrill quarrels from time to time arose between Mrs. Todgers and the girls in remote back kitchens; and sounds were occasionally heard, indicative of small articles of ironmongery and hardware being thrown at the boy. It was the custom of that youth on Saturdays to roll up his shirt sleeves to his shoulders, and pervade all parts of the house in an apron of coarse green baize; moreover, he was more strongly tempted on Saturdays than on other days (it being a busy time) to make bolts into the neighboring alleys when he answered the door, and there to play at leap-frog and other sports with vagrant lads, until pursued and brought back by the hair of his head or the lobe of his ear; thus, he was quite a conspicuous feature among the peculiar incidents of the last day in the week at Todgers'.

He was especially so on this particular Saturday evening, and honored the Misses Pecksniff with a deal of notice; seldom passing the door of Mrs. Todgers' private room, where they sat alone before the fire, without putting in his head and greeting them with some such compliments as, "There you are again!" "Ain't it nice?"—and similar humorous attentions.

"I say," he whispered, stopping in one of his journeys to and fro, "young ladies, there's soup to-morrow. She's a-making it now. Ain't she a-putting in the water? Oh! not at all neither!"

In the course of answering another knock, he thrust in his head again:

"I say—there's fowls to-morrow. Not skinny ones. Oh no!"

Presently he called through the keyhole:

"There's a fish to-morrow—just come. Don't eat none of him!" and with this spectral warning vanished again.

By-and-by, he returned to lay the cloth for supper. He entertained them on this occasion by thrusting the lighted candle into his mouth, after the performance of which feat, he went on with his professional duties; brightening every knife as he laid it on the table, by breathing on the blade and afterwards polishing the same on the apron already mentioned. When he had completed his preparations, he grinned at the sisters, and expressed his belief that the approaching meal would be of "rather a spicy sort."

"Will it be long before it's ready, Bailey?" asked Mercy.

"No," said Bailey, "it *is* cooked. When I come up she was dodging among the tender pieces with a fork, and eating of 'em."

But he had scarcely achieved the utterance of these words, when he received a sudden blow on the head, which sent him staggering against the wall; and Mrs. Todgers, dish in hand, stood indignantly before him.

"Oh you little villain!" said that lady. "Oh you bad, false boy!"

"No worse than yerself," retorted Bailey, guarding his head with his arm. "Ah! Come now! Do that agin, will yer!"

"He's the most dreadful child," said Mrs. Todgers, setting down the dish, "I ever had to deal with. The gentlemen spoil him to that extent, and teach him such things, that I'm afraid nothing but hanging will ever do him any good."

"Won't it!" cried Bailey. "Oh! Yes! Wot do you go a-lowerin' the table-beer for, then, and destroying my constitooshun?"

"Go down-stairs, you vicious boy!" said Mrs. Todgers, holding the door open. "Do you hear me? Go along!"

After two or three skilful dodges he went, and was seen no more that night, save once, when he brought up some tumblers and hot water, and much disturbed the two Misses Pecksniff by squinting hideously behind the back of the unconscious Mrs. Todgers. Having done this justice to his wounded feelings, he retired under-ground; where, in company with a swarm of black beetles and a kitchen candle, he employed himself in cleaning boots and brushing clothes until the night was far advanced.

Benjamin was supposed to be the real name of this young servant, but he was known by a great variety of names. Benjamin, for instance, had been converted into Uncle Ben, and that again had been corrupted into Uncle. The gentlemen at Todgers' had a merry habit, too, of bestowing upon him, for the time being, the name of any notorious criminal or minister; and sometimes, when current events were flat, they even sought the pages of history for these distinctions; as Mr. Pitt, Young Brownrigg, and the like. At the period of which we write, he was generally known among the gentlemen as Bailey junior; a name bestowed upon him in contradistinction, perhaps, to the Old Bailey prison; and possibly as involving the recollection of an unfortunate lady of the same name, who perished by her own hand early in life, and has been made famous in a song.

The usual Sunday dinner-hour at Todgers' was two o'clock—a suitable time, it was considered, for all parties; convenient to Mrs. Todgers, on account of the baker's; and convenient to the gentlemen, with reference to their afternoon engagements. But on the Sunday which was to introduce the two Misses Pecksniff to a full knowledge of Todgers' and its society, the dinner was postponed until five, in order that everything might be as genteel as the occasion demanded.

When the hour drew nigh, Bailey junior, testifying great excitement, appeared in a complete suit of cast-off clothes several sizes too large for him, and, in particular, mounted a clean shirt of such extraordinary magnitude that one of the gentlemen (remarkable for his ready wit) called him "collars" on the spot. At about a quarter before five a deputation, consisting of Mr. Jinkins and another gentleman whose name was Gander, knocked at the door of Mrs. Todgers' room, and, being formally introduced to the two Misses Pecksniff by their parent, who was in waiting, besought the honor of showing them up-stairs.

Here the gentlemen were all assembled. There was a general cry of "Hear, hear!" and "Bravo, Jink!" when Mr. Jinkins appeared with Charity on his arm: which became quite rapturous as Mr. Gander followed, escorting Mercy, and Mr. Pecksniff brought up the rear with Mrs. Todgers.

"The wittles is up!"

XI

Dick Swiveller and the Marchioness

RICHARD SWIVELLER, a good-hearted, though somewhat queer young man, the clerk of Sampson Brass, a scheming lawyer, often found time hanging heavily on his hands; and for the better preservation of his cheerfulness therefore, and to prevent his faculties from rusting, he provided himself with a cribbage-board and pack of cards, and accustomed himself to play at cribbage with a dummy, for twenty, thirty, or sometimes even fifty thousand pounds a side, besides many hazardous bets to a considerable amount.

As these games were very silently conducted, notwithstanding the greatness of the interests involved, Mr. Swiveller, began to think that on those evenings when Mr. and Miss Brass were out (and they often went out now) he heard a kind of snorting or hard-breathing sound in the direction of the door, which it occurred to him, after some thought, must proceed from the small servant, who always had a cold from damp living. Looking intently that way one night, he plainly distinguished an eye gleaming and glistening at the keyhole; and having now no doubt that his suspicions were correct, he stole softly to the door and pounced upon her before she was aware of his approach.

"Oh! I didn't mean any harm indeed. Upon my word I didn't," cried the small servant, struggling like a much larger one. "It's so very dull down-stairs. Please don't you tell upon me; please don't."

"Tell upon you!" said Dick. "Do you mean to say you were looking through the keyhole for company?"

"Yes, upon my word I was," replied the small servant.

"How long have you been cooling your eye there?" said Dick.

"Oh, ever since you first began to play them cards, and long before."

Vague recollections of several fantastic exercises such as dancing around the room, and bowing to imaginary people with which he had refreshed himself after the fatigues of business; all of which, no doubt, the small servant had seen through the keyhole, made Mr. Swiveller feel rather awkward; but he was not very sensitive on such points, and recovered himself speedily.

"Well—come in," he said, after a little thought. "Here—sit down, and I'll teach you how to play."

"Oh! I durstn't do it," rejoined the small servant. "Miss Sally 'ud kill me, if she know'd I came up here."

"Have you got a fire down-stairs?" said Dick.

"A very little one," replied the small servant.

"Miss Sally couldn't kill me if she know'd I went down there, so I'll come," said Richard, putting the cards into his pocket. "Why, how thin you are! What do you mean by it?"

"It ain't my fault."

"Could you eat any bread and meat?" said Dick, taking down his hat. "Yes? Ah! I thought so. Did you ever taste beer?"

"I had a sip of it once," said the small servant.

"Here's a state of things!" cried Mr. Swiveller, raising his eyes to the ceiling. "She *never* tasted it—it can't be tasted in a sip! Why, how old are you?"

"I don't know."

Mr. Swiveller opened his eyes very wide and appeared thoughtful for a moment; then, bidding the child mind the door until he came back, vanished straightway.

Presently he returned, followed by the boy from the public house, who bore in one hand a plate of bread and beef and in the other a great pot, filled with some very fragrant compound, which sent forth a grateful steam, and was indeed choice purl made after a particular rule which Mr. Swiveller had given to the landlord at a period when he was deep in his books and desirous to win his friendship. Relieving the boy of his burden at the door, and charging his little companion to fasten it to prevent surprise, Mr. Swiveller followed her into the kitchen.

"There!" said Richard, putting the plate before her. "First of all, clear that off, and then you'll see what's next."

The small servant needed no second bidding, and the plate was soon empty.

"Next," said Dick, handing the purl, "take a pull at that; but moderate your delight, you know, for you're not used to it. Well, is it good?"

"Oh! isn't it?" said the small servant.

Mr. Swiveller appeared gratified beyond all expression by this reply, and took a long draught himself, steadfastly regarding his companion while he did so. These matters disposed of, he applied himself to teaching her the game, which she soon learnt tolerably well, being both sharp-witted and cunning.

"Now," said Mr. Swiveller, putting two sixpences into a saucer, and trimming the wretched candle, when the cards had been cut and dealt, "those are the stakes. If you win, you get 'em all. If I win, I get 'em. To make it seem more real and pleasant, I shall call you the Marchioness, do you hear?"

The small servant nodded.

"Marchioness," as the reader knows, is a title to a lady of very high rank, and such Mr. Swiveller chose to imagine this small servant to be.

"Then, Marchioness," said Mr. Swiveller, "fire away!"

The Marchioness, holding her cards very tight in both hands, considered which to play, and Mr. Swiveller, assuming the gay and fashionable air which such society required, took another pull at the jug and waited for her to lead in the game.

Mr. Swiveller and his partner played several rubbers with varying success, until the loss of three sixpences, the gradual sinking of the purl, and the striking of ten o'clock, combined to render that gentleman mindful of the flight of time, and the wisdom of withdrawing before Mr. Sampson and Miss Sally Brass returned.

"With which object in view, Marchioness," said Mr. Swiveller gravely, "I shall ask your ladyship's permission to put the board in my pocket, and to retire from the presence when I have finished this glass; merely observing, Marchioness, that since life like a river is flowing, I care not how fast it rolls on, ma'am, on, while such purl on the bank still is growing, and such eyes light the waves as they run. Marchioness, your health! You will excuse my wearing my hat but the palace is damp, and the marble floor is—if I may be allowed the expression—sloppy."

As a protection against this latter inconvenience Mr. Swiveller had been sitting for some time with his feet on the hob, in which attitude he now gave utterance to these apologetic observations, and slowly sipped the last choice drops of nectar.

"The Baron Sampsono Brasso and his fair sister are (you tell me) at the Play?" said Mr. Swiveller, leaning his left arm heavily upon the table, and raising his voice and his right leg after the manner of a bandit in the theater.

The Marchioness nodded.

"Ha!" said Mr. Swiveller with a portentous frown. "'Tis well, Marchioness!—but no matter. Some wine there. Ho!" He illustrated these melodramatic morsels by handing the glass to himself with great humility, receiving it haughtily, drinking from it thirstily, and smacking his lips fiercely.

The small servant, who was not so well acquainted with theatrical customs as Mr. Swiveller (having indeed never seen a play or heard one spoken of, except by some chance through chinks of doors and in other forbidden places), was rather alarmed by demonstrations so strange in their nature, and showed her concern so plainly in her looks that Mr. Swiveller felt it necessary to change his brigand manner for one more suitable to private life, as he asked:

"Do they often go where glory waits 'em, and leave you here?"

"Oh, yes; I believe they do," returned the small servant. "Miss Sally's such a one-er for that, she is."

"Such a what?" said Dick.

"Such a one-er," returned the Marchioness.

After a moment's reflection, Mr. Swiveller determined to forego his responsible duty of setting her right and to suffer her to talk on, as it was evident that her tongue was loosened by the purl and her opportunities for conversation were not so frequent as to render a momentary check of little consequence.

"They sometimes go to see Mr. Quilp," said the small servant with a shrewd look; "they go to a good many places, bless you."

"Is Mr. Brass a wunner?" said Dick.

"Not half what Miss Sally is, he isn't," replied the small servant, shaking her head. "Bless you, he'd never do anything without her."

"Oh! He wouldn't, wouldn't he?" said Dick.

"Miss Sally keeps him in such order," said the small servant; "he always asks her advice, he does; and he catches it sometimes. Bless you, you wouldn't believe how much he catches it."

"I suppose," said Dick, "that they consult together a good deal, and talk about a great many people—about me, for instance sometimes, eh, Marchioness?"

The Marchioness nodded amazingly.

"Do they speak of me in a friendly manner?" said Mr. Swiveller.

The Marchioness changed the motion of her head, which had not yet left off nodding, and suddenly began to shake it from side to side so hard as to threaten breaking her neck.

"Humph!" Dick muttered. "Would it be any breach of confidence, Marchioness, to relate what they say of the humble individual who has now the honor to——?"

"Miss Sally says you're a funny chap," replied his friend.

"Well, Marchioness," said Mr. Swiveller, "that's not uncomplimentary. Merriment, Marchioness, is not a bad or degrading quality. Old King Cole was himself a merry old soul, if we may put any faith in the pages of history."

"But she says," pursued his companion, "that you ain't to be trusted."

"Why, really, Marchioness," said Mr. Swiveller thoughtfully; "several ladies and gentlemen—not exactly professional persons, but tradespeople, ma'am, tradespeople—have made the same remark. The person who keeps the hotel over the way inclined strongly to that opinion to-night when I ordered him to prepare the banquet. It's a popular prejudice, Marchioness; and yet I am sure I don't know why, for I have been trusted in my time to a considerable amount, and I can safely say that I never forsook my trust until it deserted me—never. Mr. Brass is of the same opinion, I suppose?"

His friend nodded again, with a cunning look which seemed to hint that Mr. Brass held stronger opinions on the subject than his sister; and seeming to recollect herself, added imploringly, "But don't you ever tell upon me, or I shall be beat to death."

"Marchioness," said Mr. Swiveller, rising, "the word of a gentleman is as good as his bond—sometimes better; as in the present case, where his bond might prove but a doubtful sort of security. I am your friend, and I hope we shall play many more rubbers together in the same saloon. But, Marchioness," added Richard, stopping on his way to the door, and wheeling slowly round upon the small servant, who was following with the candle, "it occurs to me that you must be in the constant habit of airing your eye at keyholes, to know all this."

"I only wanted," replied the trembling Marchioness, "to know where the key of the safe was hid; that was all; and I wouldn't have taken much, if I had found it—only enough to squench my hunger."

"You didn't find it, then?" said Dick. "But of course you didn't, or you'd be plumper. Good-night, Marchioness. Fare thee well, and if forever, then forever fare thee well—and put up the chain, Marchioness, in case of accidents."

With this parting word, Mr. Swiveller came out from the house; and feeling that he had by this time taken quite as much to drink as promised to be good for his constitution (purl being a rather strong and heady compound), wisely resolved to betake himself to his lodgings, and to bed at once. Homeward he went therefore; and his apartments (for he still spoke of his one little room as "apartments") being at no great distance from the office, he was soon seated in his own bed-chamber, where, having pulled off one boot and forgotten the other, he fell into deep thought.

"This Marchioness," said Mr. Swiveller, folding his arms, "is a very extraordinary person—surrounded by mysteries, ignorant of the taste of beer, unacquainted with her own name (which is less re-markable), and taking a limited view of society through the keyholes of doors—can these things be her destiny, or has some unknown person started an opposition to the decrees of fate? It is a most amazing staggerer!"

When his meditations had attained this satisfactory point, he became aware of his remaining boot, of which, with great solemni-ty, he proceeded to divest himself; shaking his head with exceeding gravity all the time, and sighing deeply.

"These rubbers," said Mr. Swiveller, putting on his nightcap in ex-actly the same style as he wore his hat, "remind me of the matrimonial fireside. My old girl, Chegg's wife, plays cribbage; all-fours alike. She rings the changes on 'em now. From sport to sport they hurry her, to banish her regrets, and when they win a smile from her, they think that she forgets—but she don't. By this time, I should say," added Richard, getting his left cheek into profile, and looking complacently at the reflec-tion of a very little scrap of whisker in the looking-glass; "by this time, I should say, the iron has entered into her soul. It serves her right."

Mr. Swiveller, it must be said had been at one time somewhat in love with a young lady: but she had left his love and married a Mr. Cheggs.

Melting from this stern and harsh into the tender and pathetic mood, Mr. Swiveller groaned a little, walked wildly up and down, and even made a show of tearing his hair, which, however, he thought better of, and wrenched the tassel from his nightcap instead. At last, undressing himself with a gloomy resolution, he got into bed.

Some men, in his blighted position, would have taken to drinking; but as Mr. Swiveller had taken to that before, he only took, on receiving the news that this girl was lost to him forever, to playing the flute; thinking, after mature consideration, that it was a good, sound, dismal occupation, not only in unison with his own sad thoughts, but tending to awaken a fellow-feeling in the bosom, of his neighbors. Following out this resolution, he now drew a little table to his bedside, and, arranging the light and a small oblong music-book to the best advantage, took his flute from its box and began to play most mournfully.

The air was "Away with melancholy"—a composition, which, when it is played very slowly on the flute in bed, with the farther disadvantage of being performed by a gentleman not fully acquainted with the instrument, who repeats one note a great many times before he can find the next, has not a lively effect. Yet for half the night, or more, Mr. Swiveller, lying sometimes on his back with his eyes upon the ceiling and sometimes half out of bed to correct himself by the book, played this unhappy tune over and over again; never leaving off, save for a minute or two at a time to take breath and talk to himself about the Marchioness and then beginning again with renewed vigor. It was not until he had quite exhausted his several subjects of meditation, and had breathed into the flute the whole sentiment of the purl down to its very dregs, and had nearly maddened the people of the house, and at both the next doors, and over the way—that he shut up the music-book, extinguished the candle, and, finding himself greatly lightened and relieved in his mind, turned round and fell asleep.

Dick continued his friendly relations towards the Marchioness, and when he fell ill with typhoid fever his little friend nursed him back to health. Just after this illness an aunt of his died and left him quite a large sum of money, a portion of which he used to educate the Marchioness, whom he afterwards married.

XII

Mr. Wardle's Servant Joe

AN old country gentleman named Wardle had a servant of whom he was very proud, not because of the latter's diligence, but because Joe, commonly called the "Fat Boy," was a character which could not be matched anywhere in the world. At the time when our story opens, Mr. Pickwick of London, and three others of his literary club, were traveling in search of adventure. With Mr. Pickwick, the founder and head of the Pickwick club, were Mr. Tupman, whose great weakness for the ladies brought him frequent troubles, Mr. Winkle, whose desire to appear as a sport brought much ridicule upon himself, and Mr. Snodgrass, whose poetic nature induced him to write many romantic verses which amused his friends and all who read them. These four Pickwickians were introduced one day to Mr. Wardle, his aged sister Miss Rachel Wardle, and his two daughters, Emily and Isabella, as they were looking at some army reviews from their coach. Mr. Wardle hospitably asked Mr. Pickwick and his friends to join them in the coach.

"Come up here! Mr. Pickwick," said Mr. Wardle, "come along sir. Joe! Drat that boy! He's gone to sleep again. Joe, let down the steps and open the carriage door. Come ahead, room for two of you inside and one outside. Joe, make room for one. Put this gentleman on the box!" Mr. Wardle mounted with a little help and the fat boy, where he was, fell fast asleep.

One rank of soldiers after another passed, firing over the heads of another rank, and when the cannon went off the air resounded with the screams of ladies. Mr. Snodgrass actually found it necessary to support one of the Misses Wardle with his arm. Their maidenly aunt was in such a dreadful state of nervous alarm that Mr. Tupman found that *he* was obliged to put his arm about *her* waist to keep her up at all. Everyone was excited with the exception of the fat boy, and he slept as soundly as if the roaring of cannon were his ordinary lullaby.

"Joe! Joe!" called Mr. Wardle. "Drat that boy! He's gone asleep again. Pinch him in the leg, if you please. Nothing else wakens him. Thank you. Get out the lunch, Joe." The fat boy, who had been effectually aroused by Mr. Winkle, proceeded to unpack the hamper with more quickness than could have been expected from his previous inactivity.

"Now Joe, knives and forks." The knives and forks were handed in and each one was furnished with these useful implements.

"Now Joe, the fowls. Drat that boy! He's gone asleep again. Joe! Joe!" Numerous taps on the head with a stick and the fat boy with some difficulty was awakened. "Go hand in the eatables." There was something in the sound of the last word which aroused him. He jumped up with reddened eyes which twinkled behind his mountainous cheeks, and feasted upon the food as he unpacked it from the basket.

"Now make haste," said Mr. Wardle, for the fat boy was hanging fondly over a chicken which he seemed wholly unable to part with. The boy sighed deeply and casting an ardent gaze upon its plumpness, unwillingly handed it to his master.

"A very extraordinary boy, that," said Mr. Pickwick. "Does he always sleep in this way?"

"Sleep!" said the old gentleman. "He's always sleeping. Goes on errands fast asleep and snores as he waits at table."

"How very odd," said Mr. Pickwick.

"Ah! odd indeed," returned the old gentleman. "I'm proud of that boy. Wouldn't part with him on any account. He's a natural curiosity. Here, Joe, take these things away and open another bottle. Do you hear?" The fat boy aroused, opened his eyes, started and finished the piece of pie he was in the act of eating when he fell fast asleep, and slowly obeyed his master's orders, looking intently upon the remains of the feast as he removed the plates and stowed them in the hamper. At last Mr. Wardle and his party mounted the coach and prepared to drive off.

"Now mind," he said, as he shook hands with Mr. Pickwick, "we expect to see you all to-morrow. You have the address?"

"Manor Farm, Dingley Dell," said Mr. Pickwick, consulting his pocket-book.

"That's it," said the old gentleman. "You must come for at least a week. If you are traveling to get country life, come to me and I will give you plenty of it. Joe! Drat that boy, he's gone to sleep again. Help put in the horses." The horses were put in and the driver mounted and the boy clambered up by his side. The farewells were exchanged and the carriage rolled off. As the Pickwickians turned around to take a last glimpse of it the setting sun cast a red gold upon the faces of their entertainers, and fell upon the form of the fat boy. His head was sunk upon his bosom, and he slumbered again.

After some amusing difficulties, which we have not space to describe here, Mr. Pickwick and his friends arrived safely at the country home of Mr. Wardle. The time passed very pleasantly.

One day some of the men decided upon a shooting trip, and Mr. Winkle , to maintain his reputation as a sport, did not admit that he knew nothing about guns. Mr. Pickwick, early in the morning, seeing Mr. Wardle carrying a gun, asked what they were going to do.

"Why, your friend and I are going out rook shooting. He's a very good shot, isn't he?" said Mr. Wardle.

"I have heard him say he's a capital one," replied Mr. Pickwick, "but I never saw him aim at anything."

"Well," said the host, "I wish Mr. Tupman would join us. Joe! Joe!" The fat boy who, under the exciting influences of the morning, did not appear to be more than three parts and a fraction asleep, emerged from the house. "Go up and call Mr. Tupman, and tell him he will find us waiting." At last the party started, Mr. Tupman having joined them. Some boys, who were with them, discovered a tree with a nest in one of the branches, and when all was ready Mr. Wardle was persuaded to shoot first. The boys shouted, and shook a branch with a nest on it, and a half-a-dozen young rooks, in violent conversation, flew out to ask what the matter was. Mr. Wardle leveled his gun and fired; down fell one and off flew the others.

"Pick him up, Joe," said the old gentleman. There was a smile upon the youth's face as he advanced, for an indistinct vision of rook pie floated through his imagination. He laughed as he retired with the bird. It was a plump one.

"Now, Mr. Winkle," said the host, reloading his own gun, "fire away." Mr. Winkle advanced and raised his gun. Mr. Pickwick and his friends crouched involuntarily to escape damage from the heavy fall of birds which they felt quite certain would be caused by their friend's skill. There was a solemn pause, a shout, a flapping of wings.

Mr. Winkle closed his eyes and fired; there was a scream from an individual, not a rook. Mr. Tupman had saved the lives of innumerable birds by receiving a portion of the charge in his left arm. Though it was a very slight wound, Mr. Tupman made a great fuss about it and everyone was horror-stricken. He was partly carried to the house. The unmarried aunt uttered a piercing scream, burst into an hysterical laugh and fell backwards into the arms of her nieces. She recovered, screamed again, laughed again and fainted again.

"Calm yourself," said Mr. Tupman, affected almost to tears by this expression of sympathy. "Dear, dear Madam, calm yourself."

"You are not dead?" exclaimed the hysterical lady. "Say you are not dead!"

"Don't be a fool, Rachel," said Mr. Winkle. "What the mischief is the use of his saying he isn't dead?"

"Mr. Tupman, We Are Observed!"

"No! No! I am not," said Mr. Tupman. "I require no assistance but yours. Let me lean on your arm," he added in a whisper. Miss Rachel advanced and offered her arm. They turned into the breakfast parlor. Mr. Tupman gently pressed her hands to his lips and sunk upon the sofa. Presently the others left him to her tender mercies. That afternoon Mr. Tupman, much affected by the extreme tenderness of Miss Rachel, suggested that as he was feeling much better they take a short stroll in the garden. There was a bower at the farther end, all honeysuckles and creeping plants, and somehow they unconsciously wandered in its direction and sat down on a bench within.

"Miss Wardle," said Mr. Tupman, "you are an angel." Miss Rachel blushed very becomingly. Much more conversation of this nature followed until finally Mr. Tupman proceeded to do what his enthusiastic emotions prompted and what were, (for all we know, for we are but little acquainted with such matters) what people in such circumstances always do. She started, and he, throwing his arms around her neck imprinted upon her lips numerous kisses, which, after a proper show of struggling and resistance, she received so passively that there is no telling how many more Mr. Tupman might have bestowed if the lady had not given a very unaffected start and exclaimed: "Mr. Tupman, we are observed! We are discovered!"

Mr. Tupman looked around. There was the fat boy perfectly motionless, with his large, circular eyes staring into the arbor, but without the slightest expression on his face. Mr. Tupman gazed at the fat boy and the fat boy stared at him, but the longer Mr. Tupman observed the utter vacancy of the fat boy's face, the more convinced he became that he either did not know or did not understand anything that had been happening. Under this impression he said with great fierceness: "What do you want here?"

"Supper is ready, sir," was the prompt reply.

"Have you just come here?" inquired Mr. Tupman, with a piercing look.

"Just," replied the fat boy. Mr. Tupman looked at him very hard again but there was not a wink of his eye or a movement in his face. Mr. Tupman took the arm of the spinster aunt and walked toward the house. The fat boy followed behind.

"He knows nothing of what has happened," he whispered.

"Nothing," said the spinster aunt. There was a sound behind them as of an imperfectly suppressed chuckle. Mr. Tupman turned sharply around.

No, it could not have been the fat boy. There was not a gleam of mirth or anything but feeding in his whole visage. "He must have been fast asleep," whispered Mr. Tupman.

"I have not the least doubt of it," replied Miss Rachel, and they both laughed heartily. Mr. Tupman was wrong. The fat boy for once had not been fast asleep. He was awake, wide awake to everything that had happened.

The day following, Joe saw his mistress, Mr. Wardle's aged mother, sitting in the arbor. Without saying a word he walked up to her, stood perfectly still and said nothing.

The old lady was easily frightened; most old ladies are, and her first impression was that Joe was about to do her some bodily harm with a view of stealing what money she might have with her. She therefore watched his motions, or rather lack of motions, with feelings of intense terror, which were in no degree lessened by his finally coming close to her and shouting in her ear, for she was very deaf, "Missus!"

"Well, Joe," said the trembling old lady, "I am sure I have been a good mistress to you." He nodded. "You have always been treated very kindly?" He nodded. "You have never had too much to do?" He nodded. "You have always had enough to eat?" This last was an appeal to the fat boy's most sensitive feelings. He seemed touched as he replied, "I know I has."

"Then what do you want to do now?"

"I wants to make yo' flesh creep," replied the boy. This sounded like a very blood-thirsty method of showing one's gratitude and so the old lady was as much frightened as before. "What do you think I saw in this very arbor last night?" inquired the boy.

"Mercies, what?" screamed the old lady, alarmed at the mysterious manner of the corpulent youth.

"A strange gentleman as had his arm around her, a kissin' and huggin'."

"Who, Joe, who? None of the servants, I hope?"

"Worser than that," roared the fat boy in the old lady's ear.

"None of my granddaughters."

"Worser than that," said Joe.

"Worse than that?" said the old lady, who had thought this the extreme limit. "Who was it, Joe? I insist upon knowing!"

The fat boy looked cautiously about and having finished his survey shouted in the old lady's ear, "Miss Rachel!"

"What?" said the old lady in a shrill tone, "speak louder!"

"Miss Rachel," roared the fat boy.

"My daughter?" The succession of nods which the fat boy gave by way of assent could not be doubted. "And she allowed him?" exclaimed the old lady. A grin stole over the fat boy's features as he said, "I see her a kissin' of him agin!" Joe's voice of necessity had been so loud that another party in the garden could not help hearing the entire conversation. If they could have seen the expression of the old lady's face at this time it is probable that a sudden burst of laughter would have betrayed them. Fragments of angry sentences drifted to them through the leaves, such as "Without my permission!" "At her time of life!" "Might have waited until I was dead," etc. Then they heard the heels of the fat boy's foot crunching the gravel as he retired and left the old lady alone.

Mr. Tupman would probably have found himself in considerable trouble if one of his friends, who had overheard the conversation had not told Mrs. Wardle that perhaps Joe had dreamed the entire incident, which did not seem altogether improbable. She watched Mr. Tupman at supper that evening, but this gentleman, having been warned, paid no attention whatever to Miss Rachel, and the old lady was finally persuaded that it was all a mistake.

Finally the visit of Mr. Pickwick and his friends came to an end, and it was several months before they again partook of Mr. Wardle's hospitality. The Pickwickians had arrived at the Inn near Mr. Wardle's place for dinner before completing the rest of their journey to Dingley Dell. Mr. Pickwick had brought with him several barrels of oysters and some special wine as a gift to his host, and he stood examining his packages to see that they had all arrived when he felt himself gently pulled by the skirts of his coat. Looking around he discovered that the individual who used this means of drawing his attention was no other than Mr. Wardle's favorite page, the fat boy.

"Aha!" said Mr. Pickwick.

"Ah!" said the fat boy, and as he said it he glanced from the wine to the oysters and chuckled joyously. He was fatter than ever.

"Well, you look rosy enough my young friend," said Mr. Pickwick.

"I have been sitting in front of the fire," replied the fat boy, who had indeed heated himself to the color of a new chimney pot in the course of an hour's nap. "Master sent me over with the cart to carry your luggage over to the house." Mr. Pickwick called his man, Sam Weller, to him and said, "Help Mr. Wardle's servant to put the packages into the cart and then ride on with him. We prefer to walk." Having given this direction Mr. Pickwick and his three friends walked briskly away, leaving Mr. Weller and the fat boy face to face for the first time. Sam looked at the fat boy with great astonishment but without saying a word, and began to put the things rapidly upon the cart while Joe stood calmly by and seemed to think it a very interesting sort of thing to see Mr. Weller working by himself.

"There," said Sam, "everything packed at last. There they are."

"Yes," said the fat boy in a very satisfied tone, "there they are."

"Well, young twenty stone," said Sam. "You're a nice specimen, you are."

"Thankee," said the fat boy.

"You ain't got nothing on your mind as makes you fret yourself, have you?" inquired Sam.

"Not as I knows of," replied the boy.

"I should rather have thought, to look at you, that you was a laborin' under a disappointed love affair with some young woman," said Sam. "Vell, young boa-constrictor," said Sam, "I'm glad to hear it. Do you ever drink anythin'?"

"I likes eatin' better," replied the boy.

"Ah!" said Sam. "I should ha' 'sposed that, but I 'spose you were never cold with all them elastic fixtures?"

"Was sometimes," replied the boy, "and I likes a drop of something that's good."

"Ah! you do, do you," said Sam, "come this way." Then after a short interruption they got into the cart.

"You can drive, can you?" said the fat boy.

"I should rather think so," replied Sam.

"Well then," said the fat boy, putting the reins in his hands and pointing up a lane, "it's as straight as you can drive. You can't miss it." With these words the fat boy laid himself affectionately down by the side of the provisions and placing an oyster barrel under his head for a pillow, fell asleep instantly.

"Vell," said Sam, "of all the boys ever I set my eyes on—wake up young dropsy." But as young dropsy could not be awakened, Sam Weller set himself down in front of the cart, started the old horse with a jerk of the rein, and jogged steadily on toward Manor Farm.

XIII

A Brave and Honest Boy, Oliver Twist

LITTLE Oliver Twist was an orphan. He never saw his mother or his father. He was born at the workhouse, the home for paupers, where his poor heart-broken mother had been taken just a short time before baby Oliver came; and, the very night he was born, she was so sick and weak she said: "Let me see my child and then I will die." The old nurse said: "Nonsense, my dear, you must not think of dying, you have something now to live for." The good kind doctor said she must be very brave and she might get well. They brought her little baby boy to her, and she hugged him in her weak arms and she kissed him on the brow many times and cuddled him up as close as her feeble arms could hold him; and then she looked at him long and steadily, and a sweet smile came over her face and a bright light came into her eyes, and before the smile could pass from her lips she died.

The old nurse wept as she took the little baby from its dead mother's arms; and the good doctor had to wipe the tears from his eyes, it was so very, very sad.

After wrapping the baby in a blanket and laying him in a warm place, the old nurse straightened out the limbs of the young mother and folded her hands on her breast; and, spreading a white sheet over her still form, she called the doctor to look at her—for the nurse and the doctor were all who were there. The same sweet smile was on her face, and the doctor said as he looked upon her: "Poor, poor girl, she is so beautiful and so young! What strange fate has brought her to this poor place? Nurse, take good care of the baby, for his mother must have been, at one time, a kind and gentle woman."

The next day they took the unknown woman out to the potter's field and buried her; and, for nine months, the old nurse at the work-house took care of the baby; though, it is sad to say, this old woman, kind-hearted though she was, was at the same time so fond of gin that she often took the money, which ought to have bought milk for the baby, to buy drink for herself.

Nobody knew what the young mother's name was, and so this baby had no name, until, at last, Mr. Bumble, who was one of the parish officers who looked after the paupers, came and named him *Oliver Twist*.

When little Oliver was nine months old they took him away from the workhouse and carried him to the "Poor Farm," where there were twenty-five or thirty other poor children who had no parents. A woman by the name of Mrs. Mann had charge of this cottage. The parish gave her an allowance of enough money to keep the children in plenty of food and clothing; but she starved the little ones to keep the money for herself, so that many of them died and others came to take their places. But young Oliver was a tough little fellow, and, while he looked very pale and thin, he was, otherwise, healthy and hung on to his life.

Mrs. Mann was also very cruel to the children. She would scold and beat them and shut them up in the cellar and treat them meanly in many ways when no visitors were there. But, when any of the men who had control or visitors came around, she would smile and call the children "dear," and all sorts of pet names. She told them if any of them should tell on her she would beat them; and, furthermore, that they should tell visitors that she was very kind and good to them and that they loved her very much.

Mr. Bumble was a very mean man, too, as we shall see. They called him the *Beadle*, which means he was a sort of sheriff or policeman; and he was supposed to look after the people at the workhouse and at the poor farm and to wait on the directors who had charge of these places. He had the right to punish the boys if they did not mind, and they were all afraid of him.

Oliver remained at the cottage on the poor farm until he was nine years old, though he was a pale little fellow and did not look to be over seven.

On the morning of his birthday, Mrs. Mann had given Oliver and two other boys a bad whipping and put them down in a dark coal-cellar. Presently she saw Mr. Bumble coming and she told her servant to take the boys out and wash them quick, for she did not let Mr. Bumble know she ever punished them, and was fearful he might hear them crying in the dark, damp place. Mrs. Mann talked very nicely to Mr. Bumble and made him a "toddy" (a glass of strong liquor) and kept him busy with her flattering and kindness until she knew the boys were washed.

Mr. Bumble told her Oliver Twist was nine years old that day, and the Board (which meant the men in charge) had decided they must take him away from the farm and carry him back to the workhouse. Mrs. Mann pretended to be very sorry, and she went out and brought Oliver in, telling him on the way that he must appear very sorry to leave her, otherwise she would beat him. So when Oliver was asked if he wanted to go, he said he was sorry to leave there. This was not a falsehood, for, miserable as the place was, he dearly loved his little companions. They were all the people he knew; and he did feel sad, and really wept with sorrow as he told them good-by and was led by Mr. Bumble back to the workhouse, where he was born and where his mother died nine years ago that very day.

When he got back there he found the old nurse who remembered his mother, and she told him she was a beautiful sweet woman and how she had kissed him and held him in her arms when she died. Night after night little Oliver dreamed about his beautiful mother, and she seemed sometimes to stand by his bed and to look down upon him with the same beautiful eyes and the same sweet smile of which the nurse told him. Every time he had the chance he asked questions about her, but the nurse could not tell him anything more. She did not even know her name.

Oliver had been at the workhouse only a very short time when Mr. Bumble came in and told him he must appear before the Board at once. Now Oliver was puzzled at this. He thought a board was a piece of flat wood, and he could not imagine why he was to appear before that. But he was too much afraid of Mr. Bumble to ask any questions. This gentleman had treated him roughly in bringing him to the workhouse; and, now, when he looked a little puzzled—for his expressive face always told what was in his honest little heart— Mr. Bumble gave him a sharp crack on the head with his cane and another rap over the back and told him to wake up and not look so sleepy, and to mind to be polite when he went before the Board. Oliver could not help tears coming into his eyes as he was pushed along, and Mr. Bumble gave him another sharp rap, telling him to hush, and ushered him into a room where several stern-looking gentlemen sat at a long table. One of them, in a white waistcoat, was particularly hard-looking. "Bow to the Board," said Mr. Bumble to Oliver. Oliver looked about for a board, and, seeing none, he bowed to the table, because it looked more like a board than anything else. The men laughed, and the man in the white waistcoat said: "The boy is a fool. I thought he was." After other ugly remarks, they told Oliver he was an orphan and they had supported him all his life. He ought to be very thankful. (And he was, when he remembered how many had been starved to death.) "Now," they said, "you are nine years old, and we must put you out to learn a trade." They told him he should begin the next morning at six o'clock to pick oakum, and work at that until they could get him a place.

Oliver was faithful at his work, in which several other boys assisted, but oh! so hungry they got, for they were given but one little bowl of gruel at a meal—hardly enough for a kitten. So one day the boys said they must ask for more; and they "drew straws" to see who should venture to do so. It fell to Oliver's lot to do it, and the next meal, when they had emptied their bowls, Oliver walked up to the man who helped them and said very politely, "Please, sir, may I not have some more? I am very hungry." This made the man so angry that he hit Oliver over the head with his ladle and called for Mr. Bumble. He came, and when told that Oliver had "asked for more," he grabbed him by the collar and took him before the Board and made the complaint that he had been very naughty and rebellious, telling the circumstance in an unfair and untruthful way. The Board was angry at Oliver, and the man in the white waistcoat told them again as he had said before. "This boy will be hung sometime. We must get rid of him at once." So they offered five pounds, or twenty-five dollars to anyone who would take him.

The first man who came was a very mean chimney-sweeper, who had almost killed other boys with his vile treatment. The Board agreed to let him have Oliver; but, when they took him before the magistrates, Oliver fell on his knees and begged them not to let that man have him, and they would not. So Oliver was taken back to the workhouse.

The next man who came was Mr. Sowerberry, an undertaker. He was a very good man, and the magistrates let him take Oliver along. But he had a very cross, stingy wife, and a mean servant-girl by the name of Charlotte, and a big overbearing boy by the name of Noah Claypole, whom he had taken to raise. Oliver thought he would like Mr. Sowerberry well enough, but his heart fell when "the Mrs." met him and called him "boy" and a "measly-looking little pauper," and gave him for supper the scraps she had put for the dog. But this was so much better than he got at the workhouse, he would not complain about the food; and he hoped, by faithful work, to win kind treatment.

They made him sleep by himself in the shop among the coffins, and he was very much frightened; but he would rather sleep there than with the terrible boy, Noah. The first night he dreamed of his beautiful mother, and thought again he could see her sitting among those black, fearful coffins, with the same sweet smile upon her face. He was awakened the next morning by Noah, who told him he had to obey him, and he'd better lookout or he'd wear the life out of him. Noah kicked and cuffed Oliver several times, but the poor boy was too much used to that to resent it, and determined to do his work well.

Mr. Sowerberry found Oliver so good, sensible, and polite that he made him his assistant and took him to all the funerals, and occasionally gave him a penny. Oliver went into fine houses and saw people and sights he had never dreamed of before. Mr. Sowerberry had told him he might some day be an undertaker himself; and Oliver worked hard to please his master, though Noah and Mrs. Sowerberry and Charlotte grew more unkind to him all the time, because "he was put forward," they said, "and Noah was kept back." This, of course, made Noah meaner than ever to Oliver—determined to endure it all rather than complain, and try to win them over after while by being kind. He could have borne any insult to himself, but Noah tried the little fellow too far when he attacked the name of Oliver's mother, and it brought serious trouble, as we shall see.

One day, Oliver and Noah had descended into the kitchen at the usual dinner-hour, when, Charlotte being called out of the way, there came a few minutes of time, which Noah Claypole, being hungry and vicious, considered he could not possibly devote to a worthier purpose than aggravating and tantalizing young Oliver Twist.

Intent upon this innocent amusement, Noah put his feet on the tablecloth; and pulled Oliver's hair; and twitched his ears; and expressed his opinion that he was a "sneak;" and furthermore announced his intention of coming to see him hanged, whenever that desirable event should take place; and entered upon various other topics of petty annoyance, like a malicious and ill-conditioned charity-boy as he was. But, none of these taunts producing the desired effect of making Oliver cry, Noah began to talk about his mother.

"Work'us," said Noah, "how's your mother?" Noah had given Oliver this name because he had come from the workhouse.

"She's dead," replied Oliver; "don't you say anything about her to me!"

Oliver's color rose as he said this; he breathed quickly; and there was a curious working of the mouth and nostrils, which Noah thought must be the immediate precursor of a violent fit of crying. Under this impression he returned to the charge.

"What did she die of, Work'us?" said Noah.

"Of a broken-heart, some of our old nurses told me," replied Oliver: more as if he were talking to himself than answering Noah. "I think I know what it must be to die of that!"

"Tol de rol lol lol, right fol lairy, Work'us," said Noah, as a tear rolled down Oliver's check. "What's set you a sniveling now?"

"Not *you*," replied Oliver, hastily brushing the tear away. "Don't think it."

"Oh, not me, eh?" sneered Noah.

"No, not you," replied Oliver, sharply.

"There, that's enough. Don't say anything more to me about her; you'd better not!"

"Better not!" exclaimed Noah. "Well! Better not! Work'us, don't be impudent. *Your* mother, too! She was a nice 'un, she was. Oh, Lor'!" And here Noah nodded his head expressively and curled his small red nose.

"Yer know, Work'us," continued Noah, emboldened by Oliver's silence, and speaking in a jeering tone of affected pity. "Yer know, Work'us, it can't be helped now; and of course yer couldn't help it then. But yer must know, Work'us, yer mother was a regular-down bad 'un."

"What did you say?" inquired Oliver, looking up very quickly.

"A regular right-down bad'un, Work'us," replied Noah, coolly. "And it's a great deal better, Work'us, that she died when she did, or else she'd have been hard laboring in the jail, or sent out of the country, or hung; which is more likely than either, isn't it?"

Crimson with fury, Oliver started up; overthrew the chair and table; seized Noah by the throat; shook him, in the violence of his rage, till his teeth chattered in his head; and, collecting his whole force into one heavy blow, felled him to the ground.

A minute ago, the boy had looked the quiet, mild, dejected creature that harsh treatment had made him. But his spirit was roused at last; the cruel insult to his dead mother had set his blood on fire. His breast heaved; his form was erect; his eye bright and vivid; his whole person changed, as he stood glaring over the cowardly tormentor who now lay crouching at his feet; and defied him with an energy he had never known before.

"He'll murder me!" blubbered Noah. "Charlotte! missis! Here's the new boy a-murdering of me! Help! help! Oliver's gone mad! Char—lotte!"

Noah's shouts were responded to by a loud scream from Charlotte and a louder from Mrs. Sowerberry; the former of whom rushed into the kitchen by a side-door, while the latter paused on the staircase till she was quite certain that it was safe to come farther down.

"Oh, you little wretch!" screamed Charlotte, seizing Oliver with her utmost force, which was about equal to that of a moderately strong man in particularly good training. "Oh, you little un-grate-ful, mur-de-rous, hor-rid villain!" And between every syllable Charlotte gave Oliver a blow with all her might.

Charlotte's fist was by no means a light one; and Mrs. Sowerberry plunged into the kitchen and assisted to hold him with one hand, while she scratched his face with the other. In this favorable position of affairs, Noah rose from the ground and pommeled him behind.

When they were all wearied out, and could tear and beat no longer, they dragged Oliver, struggling and shouting, but nothing daunted, into the dust-cellar, and there locked him up. This being done, Mrs. Sowerberry sunk into a chair and burst into tears.

"Oh! Charlotte," said Mrs. Sowerberry. "Oh! Charlotte, what a mercy we have not all been murdered in our beds!"

"Ah! mercy indeed, ma'am," was the reply. "I only hope this'll teach master not to have any more of these dreadful creatures, that are born to be murderers and robbers from their very cradle. Poor Noah! he was all but killed, ma'am, when I come in."

"Poor fellow!" said Mrs. Sowerberry, looking piteously on the charity-boy.

"What's to be done!" exclaimed Mrs. Sowerberry. "Your master's not at home; there's not a man in the house, and he'll kick that door down in ten minutes." Oliver's vigorous plunges against the door did seem as if he would break it.

"Dear, dear! I don't know, ma'am," said Charlotte, "unless we send for the police officers."

"Or the millingtary," suggested Noah.

"No, no," said Mrs. Sowerberry: bethinking herself of Oliver's old friend. "Run to Mr. Bumble, Noah, and tell him to come here directly, and not to lose a minute; never mind your cap! Make haste!"

Noah set off with all his might, and paused not once for breath until he reached the workhouse gate.

"Why, what's the matter with the boy!" said the people as Noah rushed up.

"Mr. Bumble! Mr. Bumble!" cried Noah, with well-pretended alarm. "Oh, Mr. Bumble, sir! Oliver, sir—Oliver has—"

"What? What?" interposed Mr. Bumble, with a gleam of pleasure in his steel-like eyes. "Not run away; he hasn't run away, has he, Noah?"

"No, sir, no! Not run away, sir, but he's turned wicious," replied Noah. "He tried to murder me, sir; and then he tried to murder Charlotte; and then missis. Oh! what dreadful pain it is! Such agony, please, sir!" And here Noah writhed and twisted his body into an extensive variety of eel-like positions, by which the gentleman's notice was very soon attracted; for he had not walked three paces, when he turned angrily round and inquired what that young cur was howling for.

"It's a poor boy from the free-school, sir," replied Mr. Bumble, "who has been nearly murdered—all but murdered, sir—by young Twist."

"By Jove!" exclaimed the gentleman in the white waistcoat, stopping short. "I knew it! I felt from the very first that that terrible young savage would come to be hung!"

"He has likewise attempted, sir, to murder the female servant," said Mr. Bumble, with a face of ashy paleness.

"And his missis," interposed Noah.

"And his master, too. I think you said, Noah?" added Mr. Bumble.

"No! he's out, or he would have murdered him," replied Noah. "He said he wanted to."

"Ah! Said he wanted to, did he, my boy?" inquired the gentleman in the white waistcoat.

"Yes, sir. And please, sir," replied Noah, "missis wants to know whether Mr. Bumble can spare time to step up there, directly, and flog him—'cause master's out."

"Certainly, my boy; certainly," said the gentleman in the white waistcoat, smiling benignly and patting Noah's head, which was about three inches higher than his own. "You're a good boy—a very good boy. Here's a penny for you. Bumble just step up to Sowerberry's with your cane, and see what's to be done. Don't spare him, Bumble."

"No, I will not, sir," replied the beadle as he hurried away.

Meantime, Oliver continued to kick, with undiminished vigor, at the cellar-door. The accounts of his ferocity, as related by Mrs. Sowerberry and Charlotte, were of so startling a nature that Mr. Bumble judged it prudent to parley before opening the door. With this view he gave a kick at the outside, by way of prelude; and then, putting his mouth to the keyhole, said, in a deep and impressive tone:

"Oliver!"

"Come, you let me out!" replied Oliver, from the inside.

"Do you know this here voice, Oliver?" said Mr. Bumble.

"Yes," replied Oliver.

"Ain't you afraid of it, sir? Ain't you a-trembling while I speak, sir?" said Mr. Bumble.

"No!" replied Oliver, boldly.

An answer so different from the one he had expected to hear, and was in the habit of receiving, staggered Mr. Bumble not a little.

"Oh, you know, Mr. Bumble, he must be mad," said Mrs. Sowerberry. "No boy in half his senses could venture to speak so to you."

"It's not madness, ma'am," replied Mr. Bumble, after a few moments of deep meditation. "It's meat."

"What?" exclaimed Mrs. Sowerberry.

"Meat, ma'am, meat," replied Bumble, with stern emphasis. "You've overfed him, ma'am."

"Dear, dear!" ejaculated Mrs. Sowerberry, piously raising her eyes to the kitchen ceiling; "this comes of being liberal!"

The liberality of Mrs. Sowerberry to Oliver had consisted in a bestowal upon him of all the dirty odds and ends which nobody else would eat.

"Ah!" said Mr. Bumble, when the lady brought her eyes down to earth again; "the only thing that can be done now, that I know of, is to leave him in the cellar for a day or so, till he's a little starved down; and then to take him out, and keep him on gruel all through his apprenticeship. He comes of a bad family. Excitable natures, Mrs. Sowerberry! Both the nurse and doctor said that that mother of his made her way here, against difficulties and pain that would have killed any well-disposed woman, weeks before."

At this point of Mr. Bumble's discourse, Oliver, just hearing enough to know that some new allusion was being made to his mother, recommenced kicking, with a violence that rendered every other sound inaudible. Sowerberry returned at this moment. Oliver's offense having been explained to him, with such exaggerations as the ladies thought best calculated to rouse his ire, he unlocked the cellar-door in a twinkling, and dragged his rebellious apprentice out by the collar.

Oliver's clothes had been torn in the beating he had received; his face was bruised and scratched; and his hair scattered over his forehead. The angry flush had not disappeared, however; and when he was pulled out of his prison, he scowled boldly on Noah, and looked quite undismayed.

"Now, you are a nice young fellow, ain't you?" said Sowerberry, giving Oliver a shake and a box on the ear.

"He called my mother names," replied Oliver.

"Well, and what if he did, you little ungrateful wretch?" said Mrs. Sowerberry. "She deserved what he said, and worse."

"She didn't," said Oliver.

"She did," said Mrs. Sowerberry.

"It's a lie!" said Oliver.

Mrs. Sowerberry burst into a flood of tears.

This flood of tears left Mr. Sowerberry nothing else to do; so he at once gave Oliver a drubbing, which satisfied even Mrs. Sowerberry herself. For the rest of the day he was shut up in the backs kitchen, in company with a pump and a slice of bread; and, at night, Mrs. Sowerberry, after making various remarks outside the door, by no means kind to the memory of his mother, looked into the room, and, amidst the jeers and pointings of Noah and Charlotte, ordered him up-stairs to his dismal bed.

It was not until he was left alone in the silence and stillness of the gloomy workshop of the undertaker that Oliver gave way to the feelings which the day's treatment may be supposed likely to have awakened in a mere child. He had listened to their taunts with a look of contempt; he had borne the lash without a cry; for he felt that pride swelling in his heart which would have kept down a shriek to the last, though they had roasted him alive. But now, when there was none to see or hear him, he fell upon his knees on the floor; and, hiding his face in his hands, wept bitter tears and prayed in his bleeding heart that God would help him to get away from these cruel people. There, upon his knees, Oliver determined to run away, and, rising, tied up a few clothes in a handkerchief and went to bed.

With the first ray of light that struggled through the crevices in the shutters, Oliver arose and unbarred the door. One timid look around—one moment's pause of hesitation—he had closed it behind him, and was in the open street.

He looked to the right and to the left, uncertain which way to fly. He remembered to have seen the wagons, as they went out, toiling up the hill. He took the same route; and arriving at a foot-path across the fields, which he knew, after some distance, led out again into the road, struck into it, and walked quickly on.

Along this same foot-path, Oliver well remembered he had trotted beside Mr. Bumble when he first carried him to the workhouse from the farm. His heart beat quickly when he bethought himself of this, and he half resolved to turn back. He had come a long way though, and should lose a great deal of time by doing so. Besides, it was so early that there was very little fear of his being seen; so he walked on.

He reached the house. There was no appearance of the people inside stirring at that early hour. Oliver stopped, and peeped into the garden. A child was weeding one of the little beds; as he stopped, he raised his pale face and disclosed the features of one of his former companions. Oliver felt glad to see him before he went; for, though younger than himself, he had been his little friend and playmate. They had been beaten, and starved, and shut up together many and many a time.

"Hush, Dick!" said Oliver, as the boy ran to the gate, and thrust his thin arm between the rails to greet him. "Is anyone up?"

"Nobody but me," replied the child.

"You mustn't say you saw me, Dick," said Oliver. "I am running away. They beat and ill-use me, Dick; and I am going to seek my fortune some long way off. I don't know where. How pale you are!"

"I heard the doctor tell them I was dying," replied the child, with a faint smile. "I am very glad to see you, dear; but don't stop, don't stop!"

"Yes, yes, I will to say good-by to you," replied Oliver. "I shall see you again, Dick. I know I shall. You will be well and happy!"

"I hope so," replied the child. "After I am dead, but not before. I know the doctor must be right, Oliver, because I dream so much of heaven and angels, and kind faces that I never see when I am awake. Kiss me," said the child, climbing up the low gate, and flinging his little arms around Oliver's neck: "Good-by, dear! God bless you!"

The blessing was from a young child's lips, but it was the first that Oliver had ever heard invoked upon his head; and through the struggles and sufferings, and troubles and changes of his after-life, he never once forgot it.

Oliver soon got into the high-road. It was eight o'clock now. Though he was nearly five miles away from the town, he ran, and hid behind the hedges, by turns, till noon, fearing that he might be pursued and overtaken. Then he sat down to rest by the side of the mile-stone.

The stone by which he was seated had a sign on it which said that it was just seventy miles from that spot to London. The name awakened a new train of ideas in the boy's mind, London!—that great large place!—nobody—not even Mr. Bumble—could ever find him there! He had often heard the old men in the workhouse, too, say that no lad of spirit need want in London; and that there were ways of living in that vast city which those who had been bred in the country parts had no idea of. It was the very place for a homeless boy, who must die in the streets unless some-one helped him. As these things passed through his thoughts, he jumped upon his feet and again walked forward.

He had made the distance between himself and London less by full four miles more, before he thought how much he must undergo ere he could hope to reach the place toward which he was going. As this consideration forced itself upon him, he slackened his pace a little, and meditated upon his means of getting there. He had a crust of bread, a coarse shirt, and two pairs of stockings in his bundle. He had a penny too—a gift of Sowerberry's after some funeral in which he had acquitted himself more than ordinarily well—in his pocket. "A clean shirt," thought Oliver, "is a very comfortable thing; and so are two pairs of darned stockings; and so is a penny; but they are small helps to a sixty-five miles' walk in winter-time."

Thus day after day the weary but plucky little boy walked on, and early on the seventh morning after he had left his native place, Oliver limped slowly into the little town of Barnet, and sat down on a doorstep to rest. Some few stopped to gaze at Oliver for a moment or two, or turned round to stare at him as they hurried by; but none helped him, or troubled themselves to inquire how he came there. He had no heart to beg. And there he sat for some time when he was roused by observing that a boy was watching him most earnestly from the opposite side of the way. He took little heed of this at first; but the boy remained in the same attitude so long that Oliver raised his head and returned his steady look. Upon this, the boy crossed over, and, walking close up to Oliver, said:

"Hullo, my covey! What's the row?"

The boy who had spoken to the young wayfarer was about his own age: but one of the queerest-looking boys that Oliver had ever seen. He was a snub-nosed, flat-browed, common-faced boy enough; and as dirty a youth as one would wish to see; but he had about him all the airs and manners of a man. He was short for his age; with rather bow-legs, and little, sharp, ugly eyes. His hat was stuck on the top of his head so lightly that it threatened to fall off every moment. He wore a man's coat, which reached nearly to his heels.

"Hullo, my covey! What's the row?" said the stranger.

"I am very hungry and tired," replied Oliver: the tears standing in his eyes as he spoke. "I have walked a long way. I have been walking these seven days."

"Walking for sivin days!" said the young gentleman. "Oh, I see. Beak's order, eh? But," he added, noticing Oliver's look of surprise, "I suppose you don't know what a beak is, my flash com-pan-i-on."

Oliver mildly replied that he had always heard a bird's mouth described by the word beak.

"My eyes, how green!" exclaimed the young gentleman. "Why, a beak's a madgst'rate; and when you walk by a beak's order, it's not straight forerd.

"But come," said the young gentleman; "you want grub, and you shall have it. Up with you on your pins. There! Now then!"

Assisting Oliver to rise, the young gentleman took him to a near by grocery store, where he bought a supply of ready-dressed ham and a half-quartern loaf, or, as he himself expressed it, "a fourpenny bran!" Taking the bread under his arm, the young gentleman turned into a small public-house, and led the way to a tap-room in the rear of the premises. Here a pot of beer was brought in by direction of the mysterious youth; and Oliver, falling to at his new friend's bidding, made a long and hearty meal, during which the strange boy eyed him from time to time with great attention.

"Going to London?" said the strange boy, when Oliver had at length concluded.

"Yes."

"Got any lodgings?"

"No."

"Money?"

"No."

The strange boy whistled, and put his arms into his pockets as far as the big coat-sleeves would let them go.

"Do you live in London?" inquired Oliver.

"Yes, I do, when I'm at home," replied the boy. "I suppose you want some place to sleep in to-night, don't you?"

"I do, indeed," answered Oliver. "I have not slept under a roof since I left the country."

"Don't fret your eyelids on that score," said the young gentleman. "I've got to be in London to-night; and I know a 'spectable old genelman as lives there, wot'll give you lodgings for nothink, and never ask for the change—that is, if any genelman he knows interduces you. And don't he know me? Oh, no! not in the least! By no means. Certainly not!" which was his queer way of saying he and the old gentleman were good friends.

This unexpected offer of shelter was too tempting to be resisted, especially as it was immediately followed up by the assurance that the old gentleman referred to would doubtless provide Oliver with a comfortable place, without loss of time. This led to a more friendly and free talk, from which Oliver learned that his friend's name was Jack Dawkins—among his intimate friends better known as the "Artful Dodger"—and that he was a peculiar pet of the elderly gentleman before mentioned.

As John Dawkins objected to their entering London before nightfall, it was nearly eleven o'clock when they reached the small city street, along which the Dodger scudded at a rapid pace, directing Oliver to follow close at his heels.

Although Oliver had enough to occupy his attention in keeping sight of his leader, he could not help bestowing a few hasty glances on either side of the way as he passed along. A dirtier or more wretched place he had never seen.

Oliver was just considering whether he hadn't better run away, when they reached the bottom of the hill. His conductor, catching him by the arm, pushed open the door of a house, and, drawing him into the passage, closed it behind them.

"Now, then!" cried a voice from below, in reply to a whistle from the Dodger.

"Plummy and slam!" was the reply.

This seemed to be some watchword or signal that all was right; for the light of a feeble candle gleamed on the wall at the remote end of the passage, and a man's face peeped out from where a balustrade of the old kitchen staircase had been broken away.

"There's two of you," said the man, thrusting the candle farther out, and shading his eyes with his hand. "Who's the t'other one?"

"A new pal," replied Jack Dawkins, pulling Oliver forward.

"Where did he come from?"

"Greenland. Is Fagin up-stairs?"

"Yes; he's a sortin' the wipes. Up with you!" The candle was drawn back, and the face disappeared.

Oliver, groping his way with one hand, and having the other firmly grasped by his companion, ascended with much difficulty the dark and broken stairs; which his conductor mounted with an ease and expedition that showed he was well acquainted with them. He threw open the door of a back-room, and drew Oliver in after him.

The walls and ceiling of the room were perfectly black with age and dirt. There was a deal table before the fire, upon which were a candle stuck in a ginger-beer bottle, two or three pewter-pots, a loaf and butter, and a plate. Seated round the table were four or five boys, none older than the Dodger, smoking clay pipes and drinking spirits, with the air of middle-aged men. These all crowded about their friend as he whispered a few words to the Jewish proprietor; and then turned round and grinned at Oliver. So did the Jew himself, toasting-fork in hand.

"This is him, Fagin," said Jack Dawkins; "my friend, Oliver Twist."

The Jew grinned, and, making a low bow to Oliver, took him by the hand, and hoped he should have the honor of a closer acquaintance. Upon this, the young gentlemen with the pipes came round him and shook both his hands very hard.

"We are very glad to see you. Oliver, very," said the Jew. "Dodger, take off the sausages, and draw a tub near the fire for Oliver. Ah! you're a-staring at the pocket-handkerchiefs! eh, my dear! There are a good many of 'em, ain't there? We've just looked 'em out, ready for the wash: that's all, Oliver—that's all. Ha! ha! ha!"

The latter part of this speech was hailed by a noisy shout from all the pupils of the merry old gentleman; in the midst of which they went to supper.

Oliver ate his share, and the Jew then mixed him a glass of hot gin and water, telling him he must drink it off directly, because another gentleman wanted the tumbler. Oliver did as he was desired. Immediately afterward he felt himself gently lifted on to one of the sacks; and then he sunk into a deep sleep.

It was late next morning when Oliver awoke from a sound, long sleep. There was no other person in the room but the old Jew, who was boiling some coffee in a saucepan for breakfast, and whistling softly to himself as he stirred it round and round with an iron spoon. He would stop every now and then to listen when there was the least noise below; and when he had satisfied himself, he would go on, whistling and stirring again, as before.

Although Oliver had roused himself from sleep, he was not thoroughly awake.

Oliver was precisely in this condition. He saw the Jew with his half-closed eyes; heard his low whistling; and recognized the sound of the spoon grating against the saucepan's sides.

When the coffee was done, the Jew drew the saucepan to the hob, looked at Oliver, and called him by his name. He did not answer, and was to all appearance asleep.

After satisfying himself upon this head, the Jew stepped gently to the door, which he fastened. He then drew forth, as it seemed to Oliver, from some trap in the floor, a small box, which he placed carefully on the table. His eyes glistened as he raised the lid and looked in. Dragging an old chair to the table, he sat down; and took from it a magnificent gold watch, sparkling with jewels.

"Aha!" said the Jew, shrugging up his shoulders and distorting every feature with a hideous grin. "Clever dogs! Clever dogs! Stanch to the last! Never told the old parson where they were. Never peached upon old Fagin! And why should they? It wouldn't have loosened the knot, or kept the drop up, a minute longer. No, no, no! Fine fellows! Fine fellows!"

With these and other muttered remarks of the like nature, the Jew once more laid the watch in its place of safety. At least half a dozen more were severally drawn forth from the same box, and looked at with equal pleasure; besides rings, bracelets, and other articles of jewelry, of such magnificent materials, and costly workmanship, that Oliver had no idea even of their names.

As the Jew looked up, his bright dark eyes, which had been staring at the jewelry, fell on Oliver's face; the boy's eyes were fixed on his in mute curiosity; and although the recognition was only for an instant, it was enough to show the old man that he had been observed. He closed the lid of the box with a loud crash; and, laying his hand on a bread-knife which was on the table, started furiously up.

"What's that?" said the Jew. "What do you watch me for? Why are you awake? What have you seen? Speak out boy! Quick—quick! for your life!"

"I wasn't able to sleep any longer, sir," replied Oliver, meekly. "I am very sorry if I have disturbed you, sir."

"You were not awake an hour ago?" said the Jew, scowling fiercely.

"No! No, indeed!" replied Oliver.

"Are you sure?" cried the Jew, with a still fiercer look than before, and a threatening attitude.

"Upon my word I was not, sir," replied Oliver, earnestly.

"Tush, tush, my dear!" said the Jew, abruptly resuming his old manner, and playing with the knife a little, before he laid it down; to make Oliver think that he had caught it up in mere sport. "Of course I know that, my dear. I only tried to frighten you. You're a brave boy. Ha! ha! you're a brave boy, Oliver!" The Jew rubbed his hands with a chuckle, but glanced uneasily at the box, notwithstanding.

"Did you see any of these pretty things, my dear?" said the Jew, laying his hand upon it after a short pause.

"Yes, sir," replied Oliver.

"Ah!" said the Jew, turning rather pale. "They—they're mine, Oliver: my little property. All I have to live upon in my old age. The folks call me a miser, my dear. Only a miser; that's all."

Oliver thought the old gentleman must be a decided miser to live in such a dirty place, with so many watches; but, thinking that perhaps his fondness for the Dodger and the other boys cost him a good deal of money, he only looked kindly at the Jew, and asked if he might get up.

"Certainly, my dear, certainly," replied the old gentleman. "There's a pitcher of water in the corner by the door. Bring it here, and I'll give you a basin to wash in, my dear."

Oliver got up, walked across the room, and stooped for an instant to raise the pitcher. When he turned his head the box was gone.

He had scarcely washed himself, and made everything tidy by emptying the basin out of the window, agreeably to the Jew's directions, when the Dodger returned, accompanied by a very sprightly young friend, whom Oliver had seen smoking on the previous night, and who was now formally introduced to him as Charley Bates. The four sat down to breakfast on the coffee and some hot rolls and ham which the Dodger had brought home in the crown of his hat.

"Well," said the Jew, glancing slyly at Oliver, and addressing himself to the Dodger, "I hope you've been at work this morning, my dears?"

"Hard," replied the Dodger.

"As nails," added Charley Bates.

"Good boys, good boys!" said the Jew. "What have *you*, Dodger?"

"A couple of pocket-books," replied that young gentleman.

"Lined?" inquired the Jew, with eagerness.

"Pretty well," replied the Dodger, producing two pocket-books.

"Not so heavy as they might be," said the Jew, after looking at the insides carefully; "but very neat and nicely made. A good workman, ain't he, Oliver?"

"Very, indeed, sir," said Oliver. At which Mr. Charles Bates laughed uproariously, very much to the amazement of Oliver, who saw nothing to laugh at in anything that had passed.

"And what have you got, my dear?" said Fagin to Charley Bates.

"Wipes," replied Master Bates; at the same time producing four pocket-handkerchiefs.

"Well," said the Jew, inspecting them closely; "they're very good ones, very. You haven't marked them well, though, Charley; so the marks shall be picked out with a needle, and we'll teach Oliver how to do it. Shall us, Oliver, eh? Ha! ha! ha!"

"If you please, sir," said Oliver.

"You'd like to be able to make pocket-handkerchiefs as easy as Charley Bates, wouldn't you, my dear?" said the Jew.

"Very much, indeed, if you'll teach me, sir," replied Oliver.

Master Bates burst into another laugh.

"He is so jolly green!" said Charley when he recovered, as an apology to the company for his impolite behavior.

The Dodger said nothing, but he smoothed Oliver's hair over his eyes, and said he'd know better by-and-by.

When the breakfast was cleared away, the merry old gentleman and the two boys played at a very curious and uncommon game, which was performed in this way: The merry old gentleman, placing a snuff-box in one pocket of his trousers, a note-case in the other, and a watch in his waistcoat pocket, with a guard-chain round his neck, and sticking a mock-diamond pin in his shirt, buttoned his coat tight around him, and putting his spectacle-case and handkerchief in his pockets, trotted up and down the room with a stick, in imitation of the manner in which old gentlemen walk about the streets any hour in the day.

Now during all this time the two boys followed him closely about, getting out of his sight, so nimbly, every time he turned round that it was impossible to follow their motions. At last the Dodger trod upon his toes or ran upon his boot accidentally, while Charley Bates stumbled up against him behind; and in that one moment they took from him, with the most extraordinary rapidity, snuff-box, note-case, watch-guard, chain, shirt-pin, pocket handkerchief, even the spectacle-case. If the old gentleman felt a hand in any one of his pockets, he cried out where it was, and then the game began all over again.

When this game had been played a great many times, Charley Bates expressed his opinion that it was time to pad the hoof. This, it occurred to Oliver, must be French for going out; for, directly afterward, the Dodger and Charley went away together, having been kindly furnished by the amiable old Jew with money to spend.

"There, my dear," said Fagin. "That's a pleasant life, isn't it? They have gone out for the day."

"Have they done work, sir?" inquired Oliver.

"Yes," said the Jew; "that is, unless they should unexpectedly come across any when they are out; and they won't neglect it, if they do, my dear, depend upon it. Make 'em your models, my dear. Make 'em your models," tapping the fire-shovel on the hearth to add force to his words; "do everything they bid you, and take their advice in all matters—especially the Dodger's my dear. He'll be a great man himself, and will make you one too, if you take pattern by him. Is my handkerchief hanging out of my pocket, my dear?" said the Jew, stopping short.

"Yes, sir," said Oliver.

"See if you can take it out, without my feeling it, as you saw them do when we were at play this morning."

Oliver held up the bottom of the pocket with one hand, as he had seen the Dodger hold it, and drew the handkerchief lightly out with the other.

"Is it gone?" cried the Jew.

"Here it is, sir," said Oliver, showing it in his hand.

"You're a clever boy, my dear," said the playful old gentleman, patting Oliver on the head approvingly. "I never saw a sharper lad. Here's a shilling for you. If you go on in this way, you'll be the greatest man of the time. And now come here, and I'll show you how to take the marks out of the handkerchief."

Oliver wondered what picking the old gentleman's pocket in play had to do with his chances of being a great man. But, thinking that the Jew, being so much older must know best, he followed him quietly to the table, and was soon deeply at work in his new study.

For many days Oliver remained in the Jew's room, picking the marks out of the pocket-handkerchiefs (of which a great number were brought home), and sometimes taking part in the game already described, which the two boys and the Jew played, regularly, every morning.

At length, one morning, Oliver obtained the permission to go out with the boys. There had been no handkerchiefs to work upon for two or three days, and the dinners had been rather meager. Perhaps these were reasons for the old gentleman giving his assent; but, whether they were or no, he told Oliver he might go, and placed him under the joint care of Charley Bates and his friend, the Dodger.

The three boys started out; the Dodger with his coat-sleeves tucked up and his hat cocked, as usual; Master Bates sauntering along with his hands in his pockets; and Oliver between them, wondering where they were going, and what they would teach him to make first.

They were just coming from a narrow court not far from an open square, which is yet called "The Green," when the Dodger made a sudden stop, and, laying his finger on his lip, drew his companions back again, with the greatest caution.

"What's the matter?" demanded Oliver.

"Hush!" replied the Dodger. "Do you see that old cove at the book-stall?"

"The old gentleman over the way?" said Oliver. "Yes, I see him."

"He'll do," said the Dodger.

"A prime plant," observed Master Charley Bates.

Oliver looked from one to the other with the greatest surprise, but he was not permitted to make any inquiries; for the two boys walked stealthily across the road and slunk close behind the old gentleman. Oliver walked a few paces after them, and, not knowing whether to advance or retire, stood looking on in silent amazement.

The old gentleman was a very respectable-looking personage, with a powdered head and gold spectacles, as he stood reading a book; and what was Oliver's horror and alarm as he stood a few paces off, looking on with his eyelids as wide open as they would possibly go, to see the Dodger plunge his hand into the old gentleman's pocket and draw from thence a handkerchief! To see him hand the same to Charley Bates; and finally to behold them both running away round the corner.

In an instant the whole mystery of the handkerchiefs, and the watches, and the jewels, and the Jew, rushed upon the boy's mind. He stood, for a moment, with the blood so tingling through all his veins from terror that he felt as if he were in a burning fire; then, con- fused and frightened, he took to his heels, and, not knowing what he did, made off as fast as he could lay his feet to the ground.

This was all done in a minute's space. In the very instant when Oliver began to run, the old gentleman, putting his hand to his pock- et, and missing his handkerchief, turned sharp round. Seeing the boy scudding away at such a rapid pace, he very naturally concluded him to be the thief; and, shouting "Stop thief!" with all his might, made off after him, book in hand.

But the old gentleman was not the only person who raised the hue-and-cry. The Dodger and Master Bates, unwilling to attract public attention by running down the open street, had merely retired into the very first doorway round the corner. They no sooner heard the cry, and saw Oliver running, than, guessing exactly how the matter stood, they issued forth with great quickness; and shouting "Stop thief!" too, joined in the pursuit like good citizens.

Away they ran, pell-mell, helter-skelter, slap-dash; tearing, yelling, screaming, knocking down the passengers as they turn the corners, rousing up the dogs, and astonishing the fowls; and making streets, squares, and courts re-echo with the sound.

At last a burly fellow struck Oliver a terrible blow and he went down upon the pavement; and the crowd eagerly gathered round him, each newcomer jostling and struggling with the others to catch a glimpse. "Stand aside!" "Give him a little air!" "Nonsense! he don't deserve it!" "Where's the gentleman?" "Here he is, coming down the street." "Make room there for the gentleman!" "Is this the boy, sir?"

Oliver lay covered with mud and dust, and bleeding from the mouth, looking wildly round upon the heap of faces that surrounded him, when the old gentleman was officiously dragged and pushed into the circle by the foremost of the pursuers.

"Yes," said the gentleman, "I am afraid it is the boy."

"Afraid!" murmured the crowd. "That's a good 'un!"

"Poor fellow!" said the gentleman, "he has hurt himself."

"I did that, sir," said a great lubberly fellow, stepping forward; "and preciously I cut my knuckle agin his mouth. I stopped him, sir."

The fellow touched his hat with a grin, expecting something for his pains; but the old gentleman, eyeing him with an expression of dislike, looked anxiously round, as if he contemplated running away himself; which it is very possible he might have attempted to do, and thus have afforded another chase, had not a police officer (who is generally the last person to arrive in such cases) at that moment made his way through the crowd, and seized Oliver by the collar.

"Come, get up," said the man, roughly.

"It wasn't me, indeed, sir. Indeed, indeed, it was two other boys," said Oliver, clasping his hands passionately and looking round. "They are here somewhere."

"Oh no, they ain't," said the officer. He meant this to be ironical, but it was true besides; for the Dodger and Charley Bates had filed off down the first convenient court they came to. "Come, get up!"

"Don't hurt him," said the old gentleman, compassionately.

"Oh no, I won't hurt him," replied the officer, tearing his jacket half off his back, in proof thereof. "Come, I know you; it won't do. Will you stand upon your legs, you young devil?"

Oliver, who could hardly stand, made a shift to raise himself on his feet, and was at once lugged along the streets by the jacket-collar at a rapid pace. The gentleman walked on with them by the officer's side.

At last they came to a place called Mutton Hill. Here he was led beneath a low archway, and up a dirty court, where they saw a stout man with a bunch of whiskers on his face and a bunch of keys in his hand.

"What's the matter now?" said the man carelessly.

"A young fogle-hunter," replied the officer who had Oliver in charge.

"Are you the party that's been robbed, sir?" inquired the man with the keys.

"Yes, I am," replied the old gentleman; "but I am not sure that this boy actually took the handkerchief. I would rather not press the case."

"Must go before the magistrate now, sir," replied the man. "His worship will be disengaged in half a minute. Now, young gallows!"

This was an invitation for Oliver to enter through a door which he unlocked as he spoke, and which led into a stone cell. Here he was searched, and, nothing being found upon him, locked up.

The old gentleman looked almost as unhappy as Oliver when the key grated in the lock.

At last this gentleman, Mr. Brownlow, was summoned before the magistrate—a very mean man, whose name was Fang. Oliver was brought in, and the magistrate, after using very abusive language to Mr. Brownlow, had him sworn, but would not let him tell his story. He flew into a rage and told the policeman to tell what happened.

The policeman, with becoming humility, related how he had taken the boy; how he had searched Oliver, and found nothing on his person; and how that was all he knew about it.

"Are there any witnesses?" inquired Mr. Fang.

"None, your worship," replied the policeman.

Mr. Fang sat silent for some minutes, and then, turning round to Mr. Brownlow, said in a towering passion:

"Do you mean to state what your complaint against this boy is, man, or do you not? You have been sworn. Now, if you stand there, refusing to give evidence, I'll punish you for disrespect to the bench."

With many interruptions, and repeated insults, Mr. Brownlow contrived to state his case; observing that, in the surprise of the moment, he had run after the boy because he saw him running away.

"He has been hurt already," said the old gentleman, in conclusion. "And I fear," he added, with great energy, looking toward the bar, "I really fear that he is ill."

"Oh! yes, I dare say!" said Mr. Fang, with a sneer. "Come, none of your tricks here, you young vagabond; they won't do. What's your name?"

Oliver tried to reply, but his tongue failed him. He was deadly pale; and the whole place seemed turning round and round.

"What's your name, you hardened scoundrel?" demanded Mr. Fang.

At this point of the inquiry, Oliver raised his head, and, looking round with imploring eyes, asked feebly for a drink of water.

"Stuff and nonsense!" said Fang; "don't try to make a fool of me."

"I think he really is ill, your worship," said the officer.

"I know better," said Mr. Fang.

"Take care of him, officer," said the old gentleman, raising his hands instinctively; "he'll fall down."

"Stand away, officer," cried Fang; "let him, if he likes."

Oliver availed himself of the kind permission, and fell to the floor in a fainting fit. The men in the office looked at each other, but no one dared to stir.

"I knew he was shamming," said Fang, as if this were enough proof of the fact. "Let him lie there; he'll soon be tired of that."

"How do you propose to deal with the case, sir?" inquired the clerk in a low voice.

"Summarily," replied Mr. Fang. "He stands committed for three months—hard labor, of course. Clear the office."

The door was opened for this purpose, and a couple of men were preparing to carry the insensible boy to his cell, when an elderly man of decent but poor appearance, clad in an old suit of black, rushed in.

"Stop! stop! Don't take him away! For heaven's sake stop a moment!" cried the newcomer, breathless with haste.

"What is this? Who is this? Turn this man out. Clear the office," cried Mr. Fang.

"I *will* speak," cried the man; "I will not be turned out. I saw it all. I keep the book-stall. I demand to be sworn. I will not be put down. Mr. Fang, you must hear me. You must not refuse, sir."

The man was right. His manner was determined; and the matter was growing rather too serious to be hushed up.

"Swear the man," growled Mr. Fang, with a very ill grace. "Now, man, what have you to say?"

"This," said the man: "I saw three boys—two two others and the prisoner here—loitering on the opposite side of the way, when this gentleman was reading. The robbery was committed by another boy. I saw it done; and I saw this boy was perfectly amazed and stupefied by it."

"Why didn't you come here before?" said Fang, after a pause.

"I hadn't a soul to mind the shop," replied the man. "Everybody who could have helped me had joined in the pursuit. I could get nobody till five minutes ago; and I have run here all the way to speak the truth."

"The boy is discharged. Clear the office!" shouted the angry magistrate.

The command was obeyed; and as Oliver was taken out he fainted away again in the yard, and lay with his face a deadly white and a cold tremble convulsing his frame.

"Poor boy! poor boy!" said Mr. Brownlow, bending over him. "Call a coach, somebody, pray. Directly!"

A coach was obtained, and Oliver, having been carefully laid on one seat, the old gentleman got in and sat himself on the other.

"May I go with you?" said the book-stall keeper, looking in.

"Bless me, yes, my dear sir," said Mr. Brownlow quickly. "I forgot you. Dear, dear! I have this unhappy book still! Jump in. Poor fellow! No time to lose."

The book-stall keeper got into the coach, and it rattled away. It stopped at length before a neat house, in a quiet shady street. Here a bed was prepared, without loss of time, in which Mr. Brownlow saw his young charge carefully and comfortably laid; and here he was tended with a kindness and solicitude that knew no bounds.

At last the sick boy began to recover, and one day Mr. Brownlow came to see him. You may imagine how happy Oliver was to see his good friend; but he was no more delighted than was Mr. Brownlow. The old gentleman came to spend a short time with him every day; and, when he grew stronger, Oliver went up to the learned gentle-man's study and talked with him by the hour and was astonished at the books he saw, and which Mr. Brownlow told him to look at and read as much as he liked.

Oliver was soon well, and no thought was in Mr. Brownlow's mind but that he should keep him, and raise him and educate him to be a splendid man; for no father loves his own son better than Mr. Brownlow had come to love Oliver.

Now, I know, you want to ask me what became of Oliver Twist. But I cannot tell you here. Let us leave him in this beautiful home of good Mr. Brownlow; and, if you want to read the rest of his wonderful story, get Dickens' big book called *Oliver Twist*, and read it there. There were many surprises and much trouble yet in store for Oliver, but he was always noble, honest, and brave.

Made in the USA
Monee, IL
07 July 2026